RICH...FOR TEACH

Series Editor: Paul Seligson

He...g
Students
to
Speak

Paul Seligson

Richmond
PUBLISHING

Richmond Publishing
19 Berghem Mews
Blythe Road
London W14 0HN

ISBN: 84-294-4926-4
Depòsito legal: M-15315-2001
Printed in Spain by Palgraphic, S.A.

Design	Jonathan Barnard
Layout	Gecko Limited
Cover Design	Geoff Sida, Ship Design
Illustrations	Gecko Ltd, John Plumb, Liz Roberts & Chris Ryley

Thanks to Clive Oxenden, with whom I have worked for the last six years and whose ideas have influenced much of what is in this book.

Contents

Use the chapter titles above and this chart to help you find suggested answers to particular problems connected with speaking:

PROBLEM	SEE
My students make too much noise and I lose control of my classes.	PAGE 11
My students make too many mistakes when they speak.	PAGE 13
My students aren't motivated to speak English.	CHAPTERS 3 AND 8
I'm looking for ways to exploit coursebook dialogues.	PAGE 38
I can't do pair or groupwork with my classes.	CHAPTER 8
My students don't listen to each other in pairwork.	PAGE 47
I'd like to develop my own speaking activities.	CHAPTER 11
I need simple ideas to test my students' ability to speak.	CHAPTER 14

Richmond Handbooks for Teachers: An introduction

This series presents key issues in English Language Teaching today, to help you keep in touch with topics raised in recent educational reforms. The books all contain a mixture of analysis, development work, ideas and photocopiable resources for the classroom. The key note throughout is what is **practical**, **realistic** and **easy to implement**. Our aim is to provide a useful resource which will help you to develop your own teaching and to enjoy it more.

While each of the books has been written for the practising English Language Teacher in the primary or secondary environment, they are also suitable for teachers of languages other than English, as well as for teachers of young adults, trainee teachers and trainers.

All classroom activities are designed for lower-level classes (from beginners to lower intermediate) as these form the majority of classes in both primary and secondary. Most of them can, however, be easily adapted to higher levels.

The books all contain:

- *a section of photocopiable activities and templates.* These are either for immediate classroom use (some with a little adaptation to suit your classes) or for use throughout the year, e.g. assessment record sheets or project work planners.

- *regular development tasks.* These ask you to reflect on your teaching in the light of what you have just read, and some ask you to try new ideas in the class. They are all intended to make the ideas in the books more accessible to you as a classroom teacher.

- *an index of activities.* As most teachers dip into or skim through resource books, there is an index at the back of each book to help you find the sections or ideas that you wish to read about.

- *a comprehensive glossary.* As one of the main principles of the books is ease of use, the authors have tried not to use jargon or difficult terminology. Where this has been unavoidable, the word/term is in SMALL CAPITALS and is explained in the glossary at the back. Likewise, we have avoided abbreviations in these books; the only one used which is not in current everyday English is L1, i.e. the students' mother tongue.

Although all of the ideas in these books are presented in English, you may need to explain or even try some of them, at least initially, in the students' L1. There is nothing wrong with this: L1 can be a useful, efficient resource, especially for explaining methodology. New ideas, which may challenge the traditional methods of teaching and learning, can be very threatening to both teachers and students. So, especially with lower-level classes, you can make them less threatening by translating them. This is not wasting time in the English class, as these ideas will help the students to learn/study more efficiently and learn more English in the long term.

Why don't our students speak English?

I'll never forget an experience I had at the age of twelve. I'd been away from Britain for a term, studying instead at a school outside Paris where my mother's cousin was a teacher. On returning to my first French class back in Britain, we were reading aloud around the class as usual. As it slowly came to my turn, there was a hush of anticipation as everybody waited to hear my new 'accent'. Bright red with embarrassment, close to tears from the pressure and wishing I could evaporate, I forced my way slowly through that endless paragraph. All my new-found motivation for French disappeared in an instant. Although I could speak quite well, I never wanted to speak to anybody in French again. The 'system' clearly wasn't helping me to learn to speak; on the contrary!

Like me, most readers of this book will have studied one foreign language or more at school. However, probably only a minority actually learned to say very much, and few would claim to be able to speak the language well as a result of their five or more years of study. Here are a few quotes from a range of students, past and present, about their language learning experiences.

> We don't do much speaking. It's mainly academic and quite boring.

> All we learned was grammar rules and lists of unconnected words. It never really became a language until I went to France and had to speak. That's when I learned to speak French.

> I've never been good at languages, ever since school.

> My teacher always gives me good marks but I don't know why – I can't say anything.

> I enjoyed it at first but then we got a new teacher I didn't like and who didn't like me. That was the end of that.

> I really enjoyed it and did quite well. We had oral exams and they weren't too bad because the teacher was nice.

> I was too shy and inhibited. I hated speaking in a foreign language, especially with all my friends listening.

TASK

Pause for a minute and ask yourself (or any colleagues nearby):

1 How did you get on with foreign language learning at school? Did you learn to say very much? Was/Is what you learned useful?

2 Why didn't you learn to speak better?

3 When did you really become fluent? What factors most contributed to your success?

Now look at the list on page 6 and tick (✔) the first box next to the answers that you came up with, plus any others that may be relevant.

Which of these reasons formed your experience at school?

The syllabus/methodology/classes/exams didn't focus on oral skills. ☐ ☐

The things you learned didn't seem relevant to you. ☐ ☐

You only learned grammar/formal language rules. ☐ ☐

You only learned vocabulary, not phrases or communication skills. ☐ ☐

You weren't stimulated by the classes. ☐ ☐

You never had a chance to speak either in or out of class. ☐ ☐

One or more of your teacher(s) wasn't very good. ☐ ☐

You had an awful coursebook. ☐ ☐

You had too few classes per week. ☐ ☐

There were too many students in the class. ☐ ☐

You felt too embarrassed to talk to your adolescent peers in the foreign language. ☐ ☐

You liked the subject, knew it was important and wanted to learn it. ☐ ☐

You learned enough to pass the exams. ☐ ☐

You had friends who spoke the language and wanted to learn it. ☐ ☐

You've always believed that you are 'bad' at languages. ☐ ☐

Another reason (what?) _____ ☐ ☐

Incidentally, the penultimate point is hardly true if you're a non-native teacher reading this book! Many people say they are or were 'bad' at languages, but in fact, everybody can learn a foreign language under the right circumstances.

Now imagine you're a **typical student** in one of your classes.

- Re-apply this list to your classes **from his/her point of view**. Tick or cross the second column of boxes for his/her answers about your classes.
- What do you think he/she will say about his/her experience of learning English at your school with you, twenty years from now?

It would be unfortunate if most of your imagined student's answers were negative, especially if they were very similar to your own answers. It would suggest little progress has been made in education since you left school!

Look again at your imagined student's answers. Are any of the negative ones you've ticked things which you might be able to do something about? In answer to question 3 in the first task, could any of the factors which most contributed to your becoming fluent be reproduced in your classroom?

The aim of this book is to suggest ways that you can overcome the negative aspects in the first task and help your students to learn to speak from the classes that you give. Very few students will become fluent speakers but:

… they can probably speak more than they do now

… they can easily be made to feel more comfortable with what they do know.

This book includes a range of simple, practical activities designed to broaden your own repertoire of techniques and stimulate you into helping your students to talk more in class and hopefully outside class a little too. They are all easy to implement and adapt to your situation. I hope at least some of them are new and useful to you.

CHAPTER 1

What do we mean by 'speak English'?

Both teachers and students need to be clear what we mean by 'speak English'. If you ask most secondary school students *Can you speak English?*, they'll say *No*. Some will even say *No, I can't* or *Only a little*. This is almost contradictory. What they mean is *Yes, I understand what you mean but no, I can't speak English like a native speaker*, or *I can't say in English what I'd like to*. Nevertheless, they obviously do understand and can speak some English. What they should be saying is something like *Yes, but I've only studied a little* or *I haven't had enough practice yet*, etc.

This is crucial. As a result of your work as a teacher, and what they've managed to learn at school or elsewhere, they can do what they couldn't before. This achievement should be seen in a positive rather than negative light. There are various ways in which we can help students both to achieve a good level of English and to appreciate that they have done so.

1 Define our objectives to students clearly

If students achieve all that we ask of them in the time available and pass the exams, they should emerge feeling positive about it, yet many don't. Do you and your students know what they're expected to know and be able to do/say at the end of each academic year? Do they know why you are/aren't placing so much emphasis on speaking?

We need:

… to make the aims of our courses very clear, e.g. by regularly explaining and reviewing in L1

… to define the core of what students should know from one year to another rather than leaving them to guess. How else can students who get behind or have missed classes catch up?

… ideally, to have a clear aim in each lesson too and tell students what they're going to learn each time.

2 Set realistic goals

To set speaking like a native speaker as a goal at secondary school is unrealistic, but many students aren't aware of that. The vast majority of teachers are non-natives whose English isn't 'perfect' (whatever that means!), so this would be impossible anyway. Virtually none of us, for example, will ever lose our foreign accents in other languages. However, these same non-native teachers are competent users and speakers of English. Since they have the same L1 as their students, in many ways they're also the best models for their students to aspire to as a long-term goal.

Whatever the teacher's level of English, students have to know:

… what they're going to be able to say and do

… the level expected of them

in order to:

… be able to prioritise and set themselves realistic goals

… feel satisfied when they achieve them.

Do yours?

Knowing what they've done and have still got left to do each year helps the weaker students in particular to catch up. One way to do this is to define the syllabus early and regularly to students. Many teachers forget to do this, but otherwise, how do students know what's expected of them or how they're progressing?

I always try to give my students a list like the one on PHOTOCOPIABLE PAGE 1. I take them through it in class and tell them this is what they've got to learn to understand, say and answer, e.g. in the first year of secondary school. It's up to them to learn it as best they can. Each / represents a missing word or words which the students have to remember. Although they usually write the questions out in full on another sheet, we always use the SKELETON PROMPTS in class to encourage them to memorise the phrases. We do regular pairwork from the list, either with:

… one student looking at the list and asking their partner the questions
… or the list cut up into 'cards' face down on the desk or in an envelope. Students take turns to draw a card and ask their partner the questions.

Although the weaker students ultimately have to work on it at home too, at least they know exactly what to learn and do.

I also tell students this will be the content of their **oral exam.** ◆ SEE CHAPTER 14 If they can deal with all these questions, they'll pass the course. This makes it:

… easier for students to work out what they need to know
… more likely that they will try to learn it.

It's relatively easy for you to look through your coursebook/syllabus and produce a similar list for each of your classes.

3 Make sure students know how well they're progressing

It's vital for individual and class motivation to instil a sense of progress and achievement. As students' knowledge of English increases, so too does the effort required to remember everything. Their progress becomes less measurable. Many students who may have been good at and/or keen on English as beginners often lose motivation as it gets harder and their adolescent minds wander. A lot of our time and effort needs to be spent trying to maintain enthusiasm and regularly 're-motivating' students.

As well as choosing materials and topics relevant to their age and local interests, this involves:

… setting tasks and activities at an appropriate level with a concrete outcome so students can see what they're able to do in English ◆ SEE CHAPTER 10
… you taking every opportunity to praise and encourage.

Students need to be told that they've done an activity well, even if it's only pronouncing a word correctly. It's easy to let this aspect of our teaching slip as the terms go by. We need to emphasise progress, reminding students of how well they're progressing and how much they know compared to a year ago.

4 Provide criteria for students to judge their own performance

We should, for example:

… use CONTINUOUS ASSESSMENT and tell them their marks ◆ SEE PAGE 77
… provide a simple checklist of tasks they can perform, for them to tick off and monitor what they can do (and be able to revise easily if they can't). This can be a photocopiable list of the year's work, like the two opposite.

1 For lexical groups

In English, I can say:

the numbers ____   *the alphabet* ____   *the days* ____
the months ____   *the colours* ____   *the body* ____
10 animals ____   *15 verbs* ____   *20 adjectives* ____

2 For functions

In English, I can:

describe myself ____   *describe my room* ____
describe my best friend ____   *describe my family* ____
go to a café ____   *go shopping* ____

Alternatively, students can build their own checklists at the back of their vocabulary notebooks under your guidance. Each time they've learned two or three new lexical groups or functions, help them to add them to lists.

You can also use the coursebook syllabus as a tick-off checklist at the end of each term (translate it into L1 if necessary), so they know what they can do and still have left to do each year. Wherever possible, the aim should be to make students feel good about what they do know rather than bad about what they don't. Give positive feedback wherever you can.  SEE PAGE 50

T A S K

Answer questions 1 to 5 below. If you answer *No* to more than three of them, perhaps you ought to try to change the situation, possibly by using some of the ideas above.

1 Do you know what you expect your students to be able to say at the end of each academic year?

2 Do they know? Do their parents know?

3 Are your expectations realistic?

4 Do your students have ways to measure their own oral progress?

5 Do you make a point of regularly praising and encouraging your students' oral efforts?

CHAPTER 2

Dealing with persistent problems

This chapter reflects on the main problems teachers have with pair and groupwork, and suggests some solutions.

"I've got too many students to do pair or groupwork."

In a sense, this whole book is a response to just this problem. Students can't get enough practice to learn to speak English in large classes without using pair or groupwork, nor can you help them individually without it. Of course, the smaller the class, the easier it becomes, but to continue not using small groupwork means abandoning the idea of teaching students to speak effectively.

There are no easy solutions, and each particular situation will have its own specific constraints, but many teachers resist the idea because:

... they've tried and 'failed'
... they've never really known how to begin
... they're afraid of trying something different from the norm.

The aim of this book is to show you how to introduce these techniques (already used by many teachers worldwide, even with classes of 60 who can't move from their seats), and to convince you that it's worth the effort. ◆ SEE PAGE 42
It will also arm you with enough techniques and ideas to be able to carry it through. ◆ SEE CHAPTERS 7 AND 9 Could you use any of these activities?

"There are too many different levels of ability in my class."

This is really an argument **for** rather than **against** the use of pair or groupwork. Traditional methods virtually force you to teach as if all the students were at exactly the same level, when none really are. This is usually unfair on the weaker students. Besides, what are you going to do about the problem otherwise? How else are you going to be able to give them the individual help that they need?

Pairwork allows us to individualise classes more, giving:

... everybody a chance to speak
... us the chance to monitor, listen, watch, think, breathe, and find out what students can/can't do, so we can spend more time with those who need the extra help.

It actually makes teaching mixed-ability classes less difficult because we can personalise and accommodate different students' needs much more easily. Focusing on speaking won't make the problem of mixed abilities go away, but it might help some students who are weaker at reading and writing to do better!

"As soon as I put them in groups, my students speak L1 not English."

Many teachers are unsure about when/whether to use L1. There is a checklist on page 20 of activities where the use of L1 in the classroom can be justified as both valid and useful. L1 is a valuable resource to be used minimally and discreetly like any other. Ideally we'd never have to use L1 and the higher the level, the more you can phase it out. If you're unconvinced, imagine how much **less** efficient your teaching would be if tomorrow two students arrived in your class who didn't share your L1 and you had to do everything in English all the time! A general rule is to expect students to use English as much as they feasibly can, but to allow L1 where its use promotes the smooth running of a lesson.

"My students always make too much noise."

A certain amount of noise when teaching language is inevitable. Students will always get overexcited, which is usually a sign of success. Our job is to try to make this noise productive.

A key ingredient is to avoid self-inflicted chaos, e.g. via unclear instructions or insufficient preparation. Establish routines for activities so students know what to do without being told, e.g. moving quickly and quietly into pairs or groups. Unless they settle into their new groupings quickly, they'll get distracted, noise levels will rise and headaches ensue. SEE PAGE 48

Noise control is really a question of getting students used to keeping their voices down when speaking together. This requires self-discipline, which needs training and practice. All but the most reticent students can usually be trained to lower their voices. Remind them that only their partner(s) needs to hear them, not the whole class. Some students have louder voices than others anyway, so have a quiet word with them. Noise only becomes a major problem when combined with lack of discipline (see below). Here are two simple options.

Offer students a choice

- Try a simple pairwork activity and when students make too much noise, say *Sorry, you're too noisy. We have to do something else.* Stop the activity and make them do something more traditional, preferably as boring as possible.

- After a few minutes, say *This is boring, isn't it? Would you prefer to go back to (the other activity)?* Assuming they answer *yes*, insist that they do it more quietly this time. If they can't keep the noise level down after a few more warnings, stop the activity again and return to the boring exercise.

I've found that most students can learn to keep the noise level down for a while. Students who do want to learn to speak usually put enough peer pressure onto those who don't for the class to begin to discipline itself. This obviously needs to be done several times, or at least to be threatened whenever students get overexcited, but they do learn to co-operate if we're prepared to let them.

Draw up a 'contract' to establish clear behaviour rules

- In L1, elicit from students what they want from you and write it up as a series of promises on the board: *I'll prepare my lessons, choose interesting topics which you like, teach you as well as I can, try to involve you all, be fair, mark the homework, do some songs*, etc.

- Then ask the class *What will you do for me?* and elicit the 'rules' of the class, e.g. *We'll come on time, do our homework*, but more importantly *We'll try not to make too much noise, We'll speak in English when we can*, etc. to focus on the specific problems mentioned above. If you're clever you can get them to make just the right promises!

- Help them to translate it and turn it into a 'joint contract'. Make a big fuss about signing it and ask them all to sign it too.

- Then if they 'break' their agreement later in the term, draw their attention to the contract (as they can if you break your side!). This adult approach can go down well.

SEE *THE MIXED ABILITY CLASS* IN THE SAME SERIES

"I'd like to do more speaking, but my students just won't co-operate."

A lot of the comments above also apply to discipline. If too many students can't be persuaded to co-operate, then it's probably best to give up for that lesson and return to more traditional ways of teaching. As above, try to train them by choosing between 'disciplined fun' or 'disciplined boredom'. If we can get the majority on our side, it's often possible to use them to persuade the remaining minority to 'play along', or at least not to disrupt the class.

However, even the 'perfect' teacher would have problems teaching large classes of adolescents. How students are performing in other subjects, individual personality, mood, the time of day when they come to class all affect behaviour. Sometimes students just want to be noticed and will disrupt a lesson for no other reason. In a class practising communication skills, problems will always arise. Our job is to try to channel the energy behind this behaviour into the class.

To remove discipline problems, we have to discern the cause. Are they caused by the student, the institution where they study or the teacher? To find out if you might be part of the cause of your problems, answer questions 1 to 6.

1 Are both the content of your classes and your teaching style interesting for your students or do they find them boring?

2 Do your students know what is and isn't acceptable behaviour in your classroom or are there no clear 'rules'? What are the 'rules'? Could your students tell you what they are?

3 Are you really consistent in the way you deal with students who misbehave, e.g. latecomers, those who don't do homework, make too much noise or cause trouble? Do you take the same action each time these problems arise?

4 Are you seen to be fair? We all have favourite and least favourite students but do you show excess preference to some at the expense of others?

5 Do you threaten to punish students but then not carry these threats through?

6 Are you sometimes unpleasant, e.g. not interested in certain students, shouting at them, etc.? Do your students think you are aware of and care about their individual performance?

If your answers feel negative, then perhaps you should try to do something to improve things. They're all within your control and poor performance can cause discipline problems.

A few suggestions to help deal with more reticent or difficult students:

- Use L1 to explain your methods at the start of a course, and remind students of them from time to time so that they know your aims and how they're expected to behave in your classes. It's likely to be different from the other subjects they're studying. Establish clear behaviour 'rules' and keep to them.

- Talk to individuals who are the main source of difficulty. Their problem might be something you can help with and your interest alone could trigger a positive reaction.

- Separate troublemakers. They're much more disruptive together than apart. Sit them at the front of the class where they're less likely to misbehave.

- Re-seat a troublemaker on his/her own for a while, doing something really dull. They'll either be convinced and join in or remain a problem forever, in which case they shouldn't be allowed to spoil it for the others.

- If you've tried all you know to enourage co-operation without success, follow the usual channels in your school as you would with any other serious breach of discipline, e.g. discuss it with colleagues or your superior, call for the school director's help, contact the child's parents, etc. If your school has no recognised system for dealing with problem students or even whole classes, steps should be taken to implement one.

Ultimately, for all the problems above we have to be patient but firm, taking quick action rather than suffering or ignoring them. Discuss the problems openly with students. Make them take responsibility for their own behaviour. Remember to discuss these problems with colleagues too and look for shared solutions. You'll never be the first teacher who's had these problems, nor the last.

"But my students don't want to speak English."

If students think they're never going to need to speak English, they won't try to learn. But the reverse is equally true. Assuming they have to attend classes anyway, the best way to get students interested in English is to make it relevant and to help them to speak and enjoy it as quickly as possible, i.e. build 'self-perpetuating' motivation. Indeed, it's demotivating to study a language but not to be able to speak it, as if it were something dead like Latin. ◆ SEE CHAPTER 3

"I don't have time to give them enough speaking practice."

There are rarely enough classroom hours for everything that we want to do! Remember, pair and groupwork are ways of doing the existing coursebook materials, not adding more activities to a lesson. We can still reach the same goals (satisfying syllabus requirements and exams) without having to spend **all** the class time on written exercises. If we define our job as that of trying to maximise learning and if speaking is something desirable, then we should be looking for every opportunity to create the conditions where it might happen.

"My students make so many mistakes I can't correct them."

Students who share the same L1 tend to make the same mistakes. Many of these are easy for us to predict, e.g. pronunciation, prepositions, the third person *s*, word order or other grammatical problems caused by L1 interference. Perhaps you can try to anticipate more of them, and give more controlled practice? For example, pre-teach and drill more phrases so they're more familiar before asking students to practise together. ◆ SEE CHAPTERS 6, 7 AND 10

Similar to the way we learn to play a musical instrument or ride a bike, we learn language by a process of trial and error. Mistakes are unavoidable, a natural part of the learning process and often evidence that the student is experimenting and attempting to communicate. If we're too negative about them, students won't say anything, so we need to be careful how we react.

Is your aim ACCURACY or FLUENCY? This will make a big difference.

- If it's pure ACCURACY and they're all making far too many mistakes, then the activity is probably too hard, and you should find a simpler one. But students speaking entirely accurately is unlikely at this age or level unless they're just practising a known dialogue without improvisation.

- If it's pure FLUENCY, aiming for students to use what English they do know and can say to exchange ideas and information, then making mistakes is acceptable, indeed inevitable. Here we should aim to be correcting only those that seriously stifle communication and prevent them from being understood.

- However, what they can't do accurately they can often do fluently. A more realistic goal for oral ACCURACY is to aim for the correct use of a particular language point, e.g. question formation, polite requests, or past tense verb forms, insisting they use these forms accurately and correcting all the errors you hear with them, while ignoring the other mistakes they may be making. This is the mid-point between ACCURACY and FLUENCY which most teachers try to achieve. ◆ SEE CHAPTERS 7, 9, 10, 11 AND 12 FOR ACTIVITIES

Note: Teach students this distinction, making sure they're clear about the aim of each activity, so they do them with the right focus. This makes it much easier for them to get the 'right' kind of practice.

"My own English isn't good enough."

If you can teach an English class in the traditional manner, then you have enough language to use these techniques. Try to work out exactly what language students will need to use for activities and what language you will need to explain mistakes and rules to students. Make sure you can express this language before each class (as you probably have to anyway). Your own English will soon improve. And don't forget you can use the tape as a model too.

"My students will want to say lots of things that I haven't taught them."

It sounds as if they're interested. Congratulations! This must be preferable to the alternative of their not wanting to say anything. When this happens you have a number of options.

- If it's a fun comment, either allow students to enjoy what they want to say in L1, then get back to working in English, or teach them to say it in English if you know how, provided of course they ask you *How do you say (X) in English?* I remember being much more interested in learning Russian at school after our teacher had agreed to teach us a few rude words! Moments like this can release tension and enliven a lesson.

- There's no harm in confessing you don't know everything. You don't have to translate everything for them. If it's something they really want to say, even if you do know it, you can always tell them that you don't but would like to. Ask them to find out and tell you in the next lesson.

- Always take one or two small bilingual dictionaries to class. They can save you a lot of work and encourage student autonomy. Students can look up words while you're doing something else, e.g. during pairwork while you are helping another group. Again you can pretend not to know the words, so the students can teach you. If they really believe that they've taught you a new word or phrase and that you're grateful to them, they're unlikely to forget it in a hurry!

"I tried but it didn't work. I haven't got time to keep experimenting."

Perhaps they got overexcited because it was the first time? Maybe you hadn't spelt out the 'co-operative ground rules'? Perhaps the activity was over-ambitious, they weren't linguistically prepared, or didn't understand your instructions. (You can find out why in CHAPTER 8.)

Once or twice isn't really enough. Things rarely happen overnight in language learning! Speaking together needs to become a regular feature of your classwork before students can get used to it. Although you'll inevitably have problems at first, it does get easier. The amount of linguistic preparation students need before speaking activities generally decreases as students' level improves too.

As with any other theory of teaching and learning, its success depends as much as anything on the strength of your conviction. If you believe it will work, then you can almost certainly make it work within your own context.

T A S K

Choose the problem above which causes you most difficulty and discuss it with other teachers who work in your school. What do they do about it?

CHAPTER 3

Motivating students to speak English

Cover the page and list some key points you think are necessary to motivate students to speak English in class. Then compare with points 1–7 below.

1 Make speaking English relevant

Students learn best when they're interested in what they're doing. This means that they won't speak English if:

… it feels irrelevant

… they don't want to.

We can't learn to speak English for our students; they have to learn for themselves, so a substantial part of our role is to help them to want to do so. The key word is **relevance**.

The importance of English

Students often aren't aware of the importance of English as an international language. A few initial class activities can make them interested and motivated, e.g.

- List all the pop singers and groups they like who sing in English or have English names.

- Choose and bring in a simple pop song or pop video that they like. Spend a lesson helping them to transcribe and translate it as best you can (provided they agree to memorise it!).

- List TV programmes they like which have the titles in English (if they're dubbed) or are in English if they're subtitled.

- Do the same with films, computer games and song titles.

- Ask students to tell you all the English words they already know or see regularly around the town, e.g. the names of products (*cheeseburger*), advertising (*Levi's*), signs (*Exit*), etc. Shop windows are often a good source.

- Give them a long list of words from your language to show how many are the same in English, e.g. *taxi, volleyball*, etc. Both this activity and the previous one make students think they already know a lot and learning how to say the words encourages interest in English pronunciation.

- Ask *Who's got a (brother/parent/friend) who's studying English at a private language school? Why? Do you know how much the course costs?*

- Ask students to find out if their parents would like to speak English or if they think it's a good idea for them to learn.

- Ask *What do you want to do when you leave school?* List the jobs they aspire to on the board, either in L1 or in English. Then ask *How many of these people use English in their jobs?* The list can be remarkably long, e.g. waiter, pop star, sportsperson, doctor, flight attendant, computer programmer, etc.

- Give students a map of the world with the countries marked on it where English is spoken as a first or official language. ◆ SEE PHOTOCOPIABLE PAGE 2 You could do this as a cross-curricular lesson or PROJECT with the geography teacher to help them to learn the names of countries, populations, etc.

Making English 'real'

At my secondary school most of us never believed we'd go to France or Russia but when school trips to Calais and Moscow were organised, the language became real for those who went. Extra-curricular activities like school trips to meet English-speaking people (e.g. a school language 'assistant', a foreign footballer or musician who might be locally available) or to English-speaking places or events (e.g. a musical, a local museum tour in English rather than L1, etc.), all make a difference. Students can suddenly be made to see the relevance of your efforts and that English isn't just 'a hundred words to learn a term'.

2 Include all aspects of speaking whenever possible

Speaking means listening too

Linguistically, it's impossible to separate speaking from listening. The implication for the classroom is that students have to do a lot of listening (to us, cassettes, videos and each other). The more they do, the more their interest and desire to speak will be aroused. ◆ SEE PAGE 67 FOR IDEAS

Don't forget pronunciation

In their rush to get through the syllabus, the first things teachers tend to omit from coursebooks are the pronunciation exercises. The message this sends to students is that pronunciation isn't important. But if our aim is to teach students to speak more in class then the opposite is true. An increased amount of pronunciation work is inevitable, especially in countries where the L1 is very different from English, and it can be a lot of fun. ◆ SEE PAGES 72–4

Speaking activities for homework

This can mean breaking other habits. For example, students won't learn to speak English if they only speak it in the classroom. They have to be able to practise speaking for themselves outside class. This means finding oral homework activities. ◆ SEE CHAPTER 13

More key ingredients

- Use a good, modern coursebook with topics, illustrations and recorded material at the right cognitive and interest level for your classes.
- Localise the language by introducing examples pertinent to their own lives.
- Anglicise the classroom as much as possible, e.g. posters, classroom language, an English noticeboard, etc. to surround students with English.
- Make lessons lively and enjoyable so that the language comes to life. Luckily for us this isn't hard. Given that secondary students have to study a lot of subjects 'academically', you have the advantage of being able to do something a bit different, i.e. focus on communication skills and speaking activities.

Progress and evaluation

Are your students regularly getting enough positive feedback so they can see their progress, however small? ◆ SEE CHAPTER 1

Assuming 'passing' the course is important to students, it's also important to include speaking in tests, or they won't be interested in putting in the effort to learn. If you aren't already including speaking in their 'marks', this is probably the most important single change. The test is always uppermost in students' minds and the backwash effect of having to speak to pass the course means that more class time will automatically become devoted to speaking. ◆ SEE CHAPTER 14

3 Give them the words they need

Students can't speak or interact in English either with you or each other unless you specifically teach the phrases they need in order to do so. This is an essential starting point. Here are some examples.

- At the start of a course, give each student a copy of Classroom language (SEE PHOTOCOPIABLE PAGE 3). Begin with the phrases they need to say to you (Part A). Drill them and help students translate them. Tell students to memorise them for homework.

- Next lesson give the class a test, e.g. gap-fill or jumble the phrases on the board for students to complete or order and/or ask students to look only at the translations and remember the English.

- Do the same with the language they need to speak to each other later in the course (Part B). Once they've had a chance to learn the phrases, don't allow students to use L1 for them, either with you or when they're working together. If they do, intervene. Ask *How do you say that in English?* and insist they use the English form. If you keep this up for a few weeks, most students soon get used to using the expressions. Some teachers display the phrases around the classroom walls so students are constantly reminded of them:

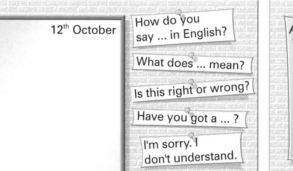

It only takes a minute to stick them up with BLU-TACK each time or you can nominate a student to do it for you.

- Don't forget to elicit more phrases either that they feel they need or that they're saying regularly in L1, and add them to the list. Teaching classroom language really increases students' expectations of using English together.

Note: This is also a good vehicle for familiarising students with a range of language structures they may not have met. The phrases provide a useful model to refer to when they do have to learn the language, e.g. *We haven't finished yet* is a useful reference when students learn the present perfect + *yet*.

4 Show them how much they can say

Demonstrate exactly what to do and say

Students won't speak English to each other if they aren't shown how. Initially, this means that you have to work harder to demonstrate exactly what they have to do before asking students to speak to each other. For example, if they're doing a pairwork activity, demonstrate what both students have to do by doing the activity yourself with a student before leaving them to do it on their own (SEE PAGE 46). This extra effort is easily compensated for as they'll then be doing all the work for the next ten minutes while they complete the activity!

Create communicative situations

Students often underestimate their oral ability, even as beginners. How often do you hear students say *I can't say that*, when what they mean is *I can't translate exactly what I want to say*? We need to put them in situations where they have to communicate so they find out how much they can say. One way I do this is by walking into class wearing sunglasses, pretending to be e.g. a Chinese tourist who speaks only Chinese or English. As soon as they speak to me in L1, I invent a few words of Chinese. When they look at me blankly, I say *I don't understand. Can you say that in Chinese, please?* Obviously they can't, so then I say *I speak English too. Can you say that in English, please?* When they see it's a game, students usually respond well and are sometimes amazed by how much they can communicate with very few words. They can do the same in pairs or small groups, pretending their partner doesn't speak a word of their L1 so they have to communicate things in English. Once students have been forced to communicate, they'll have much more confidence in their ability to do so again.

Alternatively, I walk into class and pretend to have lost my memory. I ask *Who are you? What are you doing here? Where are we? Who am I?*, etc. When students tell me that I'm the teacher, I ask *What's a teacher? What do I have to do?*, etc. for them to explain to me my job as they see it. Of course, they make lots of linguistic mistakes but the ideas that they do communicate are often intriguing! ◆ SEE CHAPTER 12 FOR MORE FLUENCY ACTIVITIES

5 They mustn't be afraid of making mistakes

The only way we can foster any FLUENCY at school is by being encouraging about mistakes. Indeed we should welcome them as a sign of effort and learning. Students can always express more if they know that their mistakes are an acceptable, perfectly normal part of language learning. Make sure they know.

6 The classroom atmosphere must encourage students to contribute with some freedom orally

Encourage students to participate

The atmosphere in a classroom affects all we do. The ideal class atmosphere is one which is fun and lively, but also positive, disciplined and businesslike. To achieve this, we need to find the right balance of:

friendliness, sensitivity and approachability
mutual respect
sharing of responsibilities
co-operation
flexibility.

There's no magic formula! But it's asking a lot for students to co-operate and speak English to each other and they need to feel comfortable in our classes and relaxed with us or speaking activities won't work.

Allow students some autonomy and choice

Students learn best when they're involved in what they're doing. The best way to achieve this with energetic adolescents is to allow them some opportunity to express their own characters and ideas. This involves taking risks, e.g. frequently inviting oral contributions from students and not worrying too much if they break into L1. If students are used to being silent in class and never allowed to talk, they certainly won't speak a foreign language together.

We need to be prepared to negotiate the content of our lessons at least a little with students, giving them choices and making sure what they're learning is of interest and some relevance to them. This will involve introducing at least **some** words which probably aren't in the syllabus. For example, have you ever asked your students *What words and phrases would you like to be able to say in English?* and then taught them those? Obscenities aside, even the least interested student can be motivated by phrases like *I love you* or *Go away!* It's very motivating to allow students to **choose** some of what they learn.

Avoid making them feel inhibited or overly self-conscious

Remember the agony of reading aloud at school? The awful peer pressure and embarrassment that many of us suffered as sensitive teenagers as we occasionally had to speak to the teacher, or answer a question in front of our friends, while they laughed at our mistakes. There's nothing more demotivating and I'd never want my students to go through my French class experience (SEE PAGE 5). The best way to defuse these tensions is to use pairwork as often as possible so speaking a foreign language becomes the norm, rather than an alien activity. ◆ SEE CHAPTERS 7–12

7 Try to be aware of the individual members of your class

We need to respond to students both collectively and individually. Speaking a foreign language requires a large effort from students and they won't make this effort if they feel it will go unnoticed. They should all feel that:

… they have the opportunity to speak

… they're making progress by doing so

… there's some reward for them if they speak

… you're really listening to them and can see things from their perspective

… you care about their progress and genuinely want them to do well.

As well as learning and using their names and speaking to them individually around the school, it's important to treat students as individuals and talk to them individually as much as possible. Spending just a moment or two with a student can sometimes shock them into making a much greater effort to learn. At least it shows that you care. We need to engineer opportunities to have time to speak to them. A good idea is to set aside one class per term or at least twice a year to counsel students individually and to discuss their progress. ◆ SEE CHAPTER 14

T A S K

Here's a checklist to measure yourself against the points raised above. If you answer *No* to any of them and you really want your students to speak English in class, read the relevant sections in Chapters 2 and 3 again to see if there's anything you might be able to do about it.

1 Do your students enjoy your classes and find them relevant?

2 Do you dedicate enough class time to speaking, listening and pronunciation work? If not, is it because of the syllabus, the exams, the materials you're using, or your choice of activities?

3 Do you set oral homework?

4 Do you give oral marks and oral tests?

5 Is English the main language in your classroom?

6 Do you teach enough 'classroom language' for students to be able to interact in English, at least to some extent?

7 Does the atmosphere in your classroom encourage students to speak to you and to each other?

8 Do you allow students to speak in L1 rather than say nothing?

9 Do you use tasks to show students how much they can communicate with very little English, despite their mistakes?

10 Do your students know the difference between FLUENCY and ACCURACY?

11 Do you invite students to suggest topics and language they'd like to study in English?

12 Did you talk individually to all your students for at least a minute last term?

CHAPTER 4

How you speak to students

You're the most important source of English for your students and also their target model of an English speaker. The speed and manner in which you speak to a class will directly effect their ability both to understand and copy you. Here we look at some aspects of the way you speak to them, but first, let's examine when we should and shouldn't use L1 in class.

1 Using L1 in the classroom

There are times when you may want to use your/the students' L1 in class.

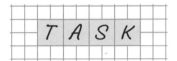

Before you read the list below, think about the times when you use/want to use L1 in class. Then check your answers with the list.

Classroom uses of L1

… providing a quick translation of an unknown word or translating texts
… explaining the purpose of an exercise
… explaining methodology
… exploring reasons why English is useful, important, etc. to motivate students
… establishing contexts, (re-)giving instructions and repairing when things go wrong
… explaining language rules
… highlighting problems and making explicit comparisons between languages
… contrasting words/sounds from L1 and English for humourous purposes
… studying texts in English and discussing in L1 with the class
… giving occasional vital information: fire instructions, test instructions, etc.
… summarising lesson aims at the beginning and end of the lesson
… allowing difficult answers from students in L1
… analysing errors
… eliciting words in English by giving students the words in L1
… rehearsing any interaction first in L1
… praising, disciplining and counselling students
… preparing for writing compositions
… using bilingual dictionaries, grammars, texts and readers
… creating interest, variety and fun

Note: One way to cut down how often you use L1 yourself is to try to identify what you regularly say in L1. Then either try to reduce it or teach students some of these phrases so you no longer have to use L1.

Some general comments about the use of L1

● Be realistic about what you expect. Having spent the rest of the day and indeed their lives speaking in L1 together, students are bound to find it both odd and difficult to change. Some L1 among them is inevitable.

● Whatever we teach secondary school students, some effervescence and overexcitement is inevitable. For them to have the confidence to try to speak to each other in English, they first need confidence in the classroom atmosphere. They need to know that every comment or aside in L1 won't cause upset or result in their being disciplined. A totally controlled classroom would not encourage the risk-taking that language learning requires. A lot of fun would disappear too. For example, students often find links between words in English and their language which can help them to remember them. My Spanish students love asking *Are you embarrassed?* because in Spanish 'embarazada' means 'pregnant' and they rarely forget the word.

- The whole lesson doesn't have to be in English. We can often start in English and then use L1 at the end to summarise or vice versa. L1 can lubricate learning. If the focus is on English and the end product is that students learn more English, even if some of the route is via L1, the activity is still valid. For example, when doing something fun like a pop video, lessons can often start in English but the activity takes over, creating such excitement that the rest of the lesson has to be done in L1. The focus, text and product are all in English and our students will usually have gained motivation for more English.

- Students, especially teenagers, need the outlet of speaking in their L1 for a moment to relieve tension, or just to assert their own personality. This is perfectly normal and should be encouraged, not suppressed. Particularly at the early stages of their learning, try to focus their energies for short intensive bursts of English and reward them for this, using L1 for relief or as a 'prize' for their efforts. For example, after students have done a five-minute pairwork activity, provided it was mainly in English, I often thank them and tell them their prize is a minute 'off', allowing them just to relax and talk to each other for a minute in L1 about anything they like. It also gives you a minute to find your place on the cassette, get ready for the next exercise, etc. After their time 'off', I ask them to come back to English and carry on. Clearly demarcating when they must talk English and when L1 is permissible makes lessons more varied and much more realistic. Students respect this sensitivity to their needs and it improves the classroom atmosphere.

- A useful way through more challenging speaking tasks is SWITCHING: students do an activity once in L1 so they know exactly what to do and what they want to say. They then repeat the activity in English (either with the same or a new partner). This L1 'run through' also provides a chance to see which words they need and to teach most of them before switching to English. Remember, we're not training students to become fluent monolingual speakers of English but effective switchers between codes, i.e. bilingual users.

- One way to cut down the amount of L1 students use is for us to listen to and react to English only. If we can ignore students speaking L1 for long enough, many will eventually give up and start trying in English. If you're convinced that students can do something in English and they're just being lazy or naughty, we should sometimes insist they repeat the activity until they do it in English. Or abandon the 'fun' and do something boring so they see what they're missing. ◆ SEE SOCIAL ENGLISH PAGE 25 AND THE CONTRACT IDEA PAGE 11

T A S K

Before you read the rest of this chapter, cover the lists below, pause and ask yourself *What advice would I give to a new teacher about how to speak to their classes, give instructions and ask questions?* Then uncover the lists and read.

2 Speaking to a class

- Speak clearly, not too fast and not too slowly. If you speak too fast, students obviously won't understand. If it's too slow, students won't get used to hearing natural English at all and won't understand anybody but you.
- Remember to use contractions. Many teachers forget this and think speaking clearly means speaking without contractions, but this can sound very unnatural and tends to produce the wrong rhythm and intonation. It also fails to provide the model students should be both hearing and aspiring to.
- Try to speak in 'chunks', i.e. say something slightly more slowly than you normally would but pausing frequently, to give students time to digest what you've said. To practise this, count *one* silently to yourself before you go on speaking after a comma or a logical word group, and *one, two, three* after a full stop, e.g. *Yesterday evening (one) I was walking home (one) when suddenly (one) I saw an enormous dog (one-two-three). It started running (one) towards me (one-two-three). It was barking (one)*, etc.
- Avoid complex language structures if you can. Try to keep most of what you say at the students' level. Many teachers speak very clearly to students but aren't understood because the language they're using is much too difficult and sometimes too colloquial.
- Use mime and gesture too whenever you can to help students understand. This makes you more visually interesting and helps to hold their attention.

3 Giving instructions

When giving instructions or explaining anything important, try to decrease the volume of what you say. Plan what you're going to say, avoid unnecessary instructions and stick to the point. Try this procedure.

- Say *Right, OK* or *Listen carefully* to draw students' attention to you. Use the same 'signal' each time you want to attract their attention so students get used to it.
- Then take a deep breath before you speak to give them time to settle down, so that when you speak, you're speaking out of silence rather than against any background noise.
- Listen carefully to what you're saying. Ask yourself *Is there anything here I really don't need to say?*
- Try to repeat any key instructions which you've given **silently to yourself** before you say them again to the class. This gives the students more time to get the gist of what you've said.
- Then repeat the instructions aloud to the class and perhaps elicit in L1 what they've got to do, to make sure they've understood. Don't be afraid to use L1 to check students understand instructions. Equally, try not to repeat yourself too much or students will come to depend on this and not listen the first time.

Note: Beware of rephrasing instructions. Although sometimes necessary, this can cause more confusion!

4 Asking questions

Here are some ways to elicit answers to questions in class.

- Ask a question and the students simply call out the answer. If they call out different answers, nominate one or two students to give their answers then elicit or tell them which is right.
- Ask a question and tell students to raise their hands as soon as they know the answer. Then nominate a student whose hand is raised to tell you the answer.
- Nominate a student by saying his/her name first, then ask the question. This ensures that the student is listening but the disadvantage is that the rest of the

class won't bother as they already know the question isn't for them. Generally it's best to ask the question first then nominate who's going to answer.

These tend to favour stronger students. With the first two, the weaker students often won't bother answering or won't have time to answer. The third technique makes them very self-conscious and demotivated if they get it wrong.

Here are some alternatives which accommodate all the class.

- Ask a question then pause for a few seconds. The students aren't allowed to call out their answer but can respond in a number of ways. They can:

  … write down their answer

  … put their hand up to show they know the answer

  … tell a partner their answer, or work it out together

  … repeat their answer to themselves silently

  … repeat the question to themselves silently several times, then decide their answer. (This really helps them focus on the question itself and tends to produce more accurate answers.)

  A combination of these techniques can be used.

- This silent period gives all the students a chance to formulate and rehearse an answer, so when you do require them to give it, they will have had time to practise it internally. The more often you allow this rehearsal time, the more confidence students will have when they give their answers.

- You can ask the question again to give weaker students another chance. Ask the question several times until everybody has signalled that they've got an answer. Then choose one student to answer and use the other students to confirm or correct this. They can vote on which is right or wrong if necessary.

There's no best strategy for questioning. We have to be flexible and vary our techniques. It is most important to:

… keep all the class involved

… avoid allowing stronger students to dominate

… avoid giving lazy, weak or shy students a chance not to answer.

Hence the alternatives above can be useful options.

Try a questioning option from the list above that you haven't used recently. Were all the students listening and able to answer?

5 Question types

We constantly ask questions in class. The type chosen directly affects students' ability to respond orally. The more difficult the question, the less likely it is that students will be able to formulate answers or speak to you comfortably. Start with questions that are easy to answer. There are four basic types.

Yes/No questions

Can you swim? Do you like playing video games?

These are:

… easiest to answer as they don't require students to produce new language, only *Yes* or *No*

… best for quickly checking comprehension and eliciting simple oral responses from students.

Note: Use these a lot if you want your classes to get used to responding to you in English. (But beware: the students have a 50% chance of giving the 'right' or 'expected' answer without comprehending at all. Make sure you use visual clues such as facial expressions and gestures to confirm that the student has understood the question.)

Either/or questions

Do you live in a house or a flat? Would you like coke or orange juice?

These are:

- … quite easy to answer as students only have to choose an alternative word or phrase from the question itself, e.g. *A flat, Orange juice (please).*
- … very useful for initiating students into formulating simple phrases. (But see the **note** above.)

Wh- questions

Where do you live? What would like to drink? How did you get there?

These are:

- … much harder to answer as students have to produce words which aren't in the question, e.g. *In Paris, Orange juice (please), By bus.*
- … also difficult to answer because we often use them to drill structures and sentence formation, asking for a full answer, i.e. *I live in Paris, I'd like an orange juice, please.*
- … harder still when we ask a more open question like *What did you do before you came to school today?*

Note: Begin to use questions like these only when students are ready and able to formulate the answers.

Open questions

Tell me about (your typical day/family/hobbies). Describe (your bedroom). How about you (Laura)?

These are:

- … typical 'prompt' questions we use to elicit language from students, but not a grammatical 'type' like the ones above
- … much more difficult for students to answer fluently.

Note: Use only when students are able to formulate some kind of answer or their confidence will be harmed.

A good strategy for balancing mixed-ability classes is to base your choice of question type on the level of the student, e.g. ask stronger students the more difficult question types.

If possible, take a cassette recorder to class and record yourself during a section of the lesson when you're giving instructions and/or asking questions. Then listen to it after class and answer these questions.

1 Were the instructions clear/economical? Could you have used fewer words?

2 Are you using a range of question types? Are your questions easy to answer?

3 Did any of your students who couldn't answer 'fail' to do so because the question was too hard?

6 Social English

A lot of our classroom language and the words/phrases each of us tend to say a lot are the words students best pick up and remember. By using English most or all of the time in class, you give students vital listening practice and the opportunity to respond naturally to spoken English. It also changes the class atmosphere considerably, allowing you to:

… establish much more personal contact with the class in English, breaking down some of the traditional teacher/student barriers

… help students begin to feel that English is a real communicative tool, not just something in the coursebook.

There are many opportunities to use English in real ways in the classroom (and outside), listed below from easy to more difficult:

… greeting students and saying goodbye
… checking attendance
… praise, encouragement and discipline, e.g. *Well done! That's better. Be quiet.*
… giving general instructions, e.g. *Can you clean the board/open the window/close the door/come to the front?*
… giving specific instructions, e.g. *Turn to page 00, Work in pairs.*
… taking the answers to tasks, e.g. *What's the answer to number 2?*
… checking others agree with the answers, e.g. *Is that right? Do you agree?*
… setting homework
… organising seating and book-sharing
… asking about absentees, why they've forgotten their pens/books, etc.
… dealing with late-comers
… talking about what they did the day/lesson before
… talking about what they're going to do later/at the weekend.

For all the above you should use English most of the time with your students. The first six to eight can be used from the start. Remember: you're the most important source of language they have. You're also the model to which they can most easily aspire because you have done what they're trying to do, which is learn to speak English.

Tick the items on the list above that you always do in English. Try using it for some of the others. Then compare notes with a colleague to see which language they use for these functions.

Note: A lot of social 'chat' is in the past tense, which is a good reason for teaching the past simple early, e.g. before the present continuous. Even if you don't want to introduce the whole tense, it's a good idea to teach and regularly use a few phrases that students can deal with:

T: *Did you have a good weekend/holiday/party?*
S1:   *Yes, thanks.*
T: *What did you do?*
S1:   *(I went to) the cinema and a party.*
T: *Good. Did anybody watch (the match/film) on TV?*
SS: *Yes.*
T: *Did you enjoy it?*
SS: *Yes.*
T: *Me too. What did you do last night, Sophie?, etc.*

CHAPTER 5

Presenting language orally

There are many ways to introduce new language in class, e.g.

... straight translation via teacher or dictionary

... the use of pictures, reading or listening

... a deductive grammar presentation from example sentences (e.g. in a coursebook)

... teacher-led activities involving FLASHCARDS, objects, mime, the board, etc.

Some presentation techniques are much more suited to encouraging oral participation than others. Below are a few tips and ideas that have helped me to get my students more involved orally. They also provide variety and are more memorable for students.

T A S K Before you read, stop for a minute and answer the following questions.

1 What's your favourite way to present new language?

2 What are the factors that make it a good language presentation?

1 'Heads-up' presentations tend to work best

When students have their heads down in their books, it's difficult to be sure they're all focusing on the same thing or following at the same speed. Indeed, they often aren't. Also, the coursebook content is often not locally relevant or interesting. So, language presentations at lower levels are often most effective with books closed and students following a teacher-led activity, preferably with you being extrovert to command their attention. The whole class can have their heads up and listen to you, looking at you, the board or other visual aids you may have. Hopefully you'll be able to provide something fun, which is aimed at the right cognitive level and is more locally relevant. There's nothing more motivating than the teacher putting on a show.

2 Don't ask students to speak too soon

Don't underestimate the importance of allowing students enough time to listen to new language before forcing them to use it. If they neither understand nor are comfortable with words or phrases, they won't enjoy being forced to say them. Part of our job as teachers is to allow a period of 'silent language acquisition' in class. (Think how long it takes a baby to learn its L1.) This requires a lot of listening practice, which is obviously difficult given our time constraints of only two or three classes a week. So, model new language a lot yourself, repeating new words and phrases several times before asking students to say them, as well as relying on the cassette. ◆ SEE PAGE 34 FOR 'MOOD DRILLS'

3 Be as visual as possible

An image, mime or object usually makes the meaning instantly clear. They allow students to see at once what they have to say and eliminate any need for translation. They also provide instant motivation for students to say the words. You should be using most of the following regularly:

... photos and pictures cut out from magazines; build a library and cover your best ones with plastic for long life

... home-drawn pictures (SEE PAGE 29), which you can use to present most structures

… realia (e.g. classroom furniture and real objects which you can bring into class: the contents of your handbag, items from the staff room, your home, etc.).

Note: Students will happily bring many of these things in for you if you ask them to, so you can build up a collection of useful language practice objects, e.g. egg boxes, empty pots, jars, cans, cereal packets.

1 Which of the above have you asked students to draw or supply for you?

2 Is there room in your staff room for you and your colleagues to store a collection of English 'realia' and/or a drawer for sets of FLASHCARDS?

4 Elicit all you can from students

In a busy, stressful job like teaching, it's easy to forget to use and remind students of what they already know. Instead, teachers tend to plough on through the coursebook or syllabus, giving more attention to what's new than to what's known. However, if you want students to speak in class, an easy way is to ask them to give you/BRAINSTORM any words or phrases that they already know. This process of asking students for their ideas and suggestions is called *eliciting*. This is a crucial way to get students interested and involved.

Here are some ideas.

- Before you introduce any new set of words (more parts of the body, adjectives or irregular past tense forms, etc.), ask students to tell you all those that they already know and write those that they come up with on the board.

- Use a picture to set up a scene, e.g. from the coursebook, like the one below.

- Ask students to cover the text and focus only on the pictures. Ask *What can you see? How many people are there? What are they doing? What are they wearing? How old do you think they are?* etc. (At a higher level, students can ask each other these kind of questions in small groups with only one of them able to see the picture.)

- Before students read or hear any text with a clear setting (e.g. Shopping, At the doctor's, etc.) or a clear topic (e.g. Elephants, Housing, etc.), ask students to take a minute together to predict in English any of the ideas/words they might find in the text. They can also BRAINSTORM in L1 and you then help them translate the words they want to say.

The key factor is not to accept in L1 what they can say in English. If you do this too often, students will never be challenged to remember what they're supposed to know. Nor will they bother anyway if they know they can get away with L1. If they say something to you in L1 which they can say in English, insist they say it in English before moving on. Although hard at first, the dividend is high if you're prepared to stick at it.

Glimpse and remember

- Tell students to look at a coursebook photo for a short time, e.g. only ten seconds. (Try it yourself: look at the first picture on PHOTOCOPIABLE PAGE 8 for ten seconds, then answer the questions below from memory.)

- Then tell them to close their books and discuss the answers to these questions in pairs. (Ask the questions orally or put them on the board.)
  What's the scene in the picture? How many people/animals are in it? Who are they? Where are they? What objects can you see? Where are they?

- When they've remembered all they can, ask them to do one of the following:
  … tell you the answers to the questions
  … simply open their books to check
  … glimpse again for another ten seconds, then close their books again and remind each other of what they missed the first time.

  Focusing on and talking about the illustration for a text gets students involved, raising interest and attention before they hear or read it.

Presentation techniques that really work

To illustrate good techniques, here are three oral presentations for:
… the irregular past tense – questions and affirmative
… the regular past tense – affirmative
… the present simple and tense-switching (past and future).

Dialogue-building

My favourite way to introduce dialogue is by building it up on the board. It was the first technique I ever learned and it still works! Below is a typical example I use to introduce irregular past tense forms.

- Draw two 'talking heads' on the board, as below. Ask the class *What are their names?* and write the best ones under the heads.

- Write the first line of dialogue as a prompt: *What/do last night?* Use a slash (/) as a regular system to signal that some words are missing and make sure students know this. Try to elicit the first line in full: *What did you do last night?* Students can usually come up with *What do you do?* so elicit or teach them the past tense form *did*. Drill as necessary.

- Then focus on the answer. From the prompt *out* elicit/teach *I went out.* Drill the question and answer between students, then move on to the next line *Where did you go?*, as below.

Build up the whole dialogue, pausing after every two lines to get students to practise the whole thing in pairs from the beginning again, one as Tom, the other as Nicole, and then swap roles. When you reach the name of the film, ask the students to suggest which film she saw and replace the *???* on the board with the name.

- You can keep going indefinitely, e.g. *What was it like? (What/like?)* and eliciting an opinion, then *What did you do after that? (What/do after that?)*, etc.

- When students have practised the whole dialogue and played both roles, ask them to remember and write it in pairs, then put the correct version on the board for them to check their work. Alternatively, elicit it line by line straight onto the board for them to copy. Ask students to spell any tricky words.

- Students can then try to personalise the dialogue, asking first you and then each other about last night.

- Don't forget to revise it next lesson and again a few weeks later if you want them to remember it. Make the prompts different the second time, e.g.

This technique works for any dialogue, whether functional (e.g. Buying a train ticket, At a hotel reception, Phoning) or structural (*What time do you get up in the morning? What are you doing tonight?*) because it's lively and fun. Students are actively involved in the build-up and practice and it provides a memorable and personal learning experience. ◆ SEE PAGES 38–40 FOR MORE ON DIALOGUES

Picture stories

A great way to present narrative is with a picture story. Here are two examples. They can both be drawn on the blackboard frame by frame. Alternatively, draw/ask a friend to draw them on FLASHCARDS, BLU-TACKING a frame at a time on the board. It's also useful to have a photocopy to be able to revise a few lessons later without having to draw them all over again. ◆ SEE PHOTOCOPIABLE PAGE 4

The day Dick disappeared

This is how I always introduce the past tense regular verbs on the board.

- Draw the first picture on the board. Say *This is Dick* and teach students to say *Yesterday afternoon Dick rushed home*. Drill as necessary.

- Then draw the second picture and ask *What happened next?* to elicit or teach *Then he packed his bags …* Again drill as necessary.

- Ask one or two students to tell you about both pictures while you draw the third one. Then elicit *… and kissed his wife.* Drill as necessary.

- Then ask students in pairs to retell the story to each other while you draw the fourth picture, etc. As you add on a picture, ask an individual student to retell it from the beginning to give you time to draw. When you get to the end of columns 2 and 3, ask students to retell it in pairs, from the beginning.

Key

Column 1	Column 2	Column 3
Yesterday afternoon Dick **rushed** home.	Then he **called** a taxi.	When the plane **landed** …
Then he **packed** his bags …	When he **arrived** at the airport …	… he **rented** a car.
… and **kissed** his wife goodbye.	… he **changed** some money.	Then he **waited** for eight hours.

And then, he **disappeared.**

- Ask *Where do you think he went? Why did he 'disappear'? Do you think his wife knew where he was? Which country do you think he went to? Why did he wait at the airport? Who did he wait for?*, etc. to build up a story. Students can come up with, e.g. *He ran away to meet a lover who didn't turn up at the airport so he couldn't face going home again, or else went off to look for her. He was a spy on a secret mission. He waited for eight hours to make sure he wasn't being followed*, etc. Settle on the version which they like best.

- Then ask *Why's the story in three columns, 1, 2 and 3?* They don't usually know, so point at and elicit the verb for each picture: *rushed, packed, kissed,* etc. Exaggerate the endings of each verb to see if they can spot the difference, e.g. mime, pretending to spit on the floor for the /t/ ending! The answer is that each column has a different pronunciation pattern.
  Column 1 = /t/ rush**ed** pack**ed** kiss**ed**
  Column 2 = /d/ call**ed** arriv**ed** chang**ed**
  Column 3 = /ɪd/ land**ed** rent**ed** wait**ed**
  Picture 10 (not in a column) = And then, he disappear**ed**. (/d/)

- If you feel it's necessary, elicit more examples for each pattern. Ask students in pairs to write up the story in three paragraphs. Monitor and write up any common spelling errors on the board. Tell students to memorise it at home as a model to guide them towards correct pronunciation of all regular past tense forms. Test them on it next lesson and again a few weeks later. You could even include retelling it as part of their final or oral evaluation. ◆ SEE CHAPTER 14

Daily routine (present, past and 'going to' future)

The picture for this story is on PHOTOCOPIABLE PAGE 5 and reduced opposite.

- Draw it (or ask a friend who can draw to do it for you) onto FLASHCARDS so you can use it again and again. Show them one at a time to students and stick them up on the board. Draw it straight onto the board if you've got the time and confidence.

- Then elicit this story. Ask the students to supply a funny name for the character to endear them to him.

  Every Monday (Skinny) gets up at seven o'clock. Then he goes to the bathroom and has a shower. After that he goes downstairs to the kitchen and has breakfast with his family. He has fruit juice and cereal. He leaves home at eight o'clock and goes to school by bus. He arrives at school at five to nine. He studies from nine to half past three. For lunch, he has fish and chips. After school, he goes to the park and plays basketball with his friends. Then he goes home and does his homework. He has dinner at half past seven. After dinner he watches TV, listens to the radio or reads. Finally, he goes to bed at about eleven o'clock.

- Revise it two or three times to help students to memorise it. When it's time to introduce the past tense, use it again to elicit the same story in the past.
  ***Last** Monday (Skinny) **got up** at seven o'clock. Then he **went** to the bathroom and **had** a shower. After that he **went** downstairs to the kitchen and **had** breakfast with his family. He **had** fruit juice ...*

- Repeat this procedure once more in the future when you present *going to*.
  ***Next** Monday (Skinny)'s **going to get up** at seven o'clock. Then he's **going to go** to the bathroom and **have** a shower. After that he's **going to go** downstairs to the kitchen and **have** breakfast with his family. He's **going to have** ...*

This is good for question and answer practice too. In pairs, one student turns over the paper and their partner asks three questions to test his/her memory in the appropriate tense. Then they swap roles. It's also a great trigger for them to personalise the language, telling a partner a version of their own day from the picture model: *I usually get up at ...*, etc.

I include retelling it in one of the tenses (without telling them which it'll be) as part of their end-of-year oral evaluation. This helps to motivate them to learn it.

Note: I've used a boy/man in both stories only because they're easier/quicker to draw. Change to a girl/woman by adding longer hair and a skirt if you want to!

Picture stories get students talking and avoid the need for translation. It really isn't hard to think of stories which you can reduce to about ten frames and draw, e.g. film plots, classics like *Romeo and Juliet, Frankenstein, Dracula, Love Story*, etc. You can always ask a friend who can draw to help you (or ask students to draw the main scenes from a film or story they've liked for you, either on an A4 sheet and/or on FLASHCARDS) then to teach them to say it in English.

T A S K

Try either a dialogue-building or one of the picture story ideas above. Then tell another English teacher about what did or didn't work to see if together you can come up with any improvements.

CHAPTER 6

Teacher-led oral repetition drills

In Chapter 3 we saw that students need to hear new language several times and that we shouldn't force them to produce it too soon. The next three chapters look at techniques for initial controlled production through oral drills.

These provide essential basic practice:

... **physically**, allowing students to get their mouths and tongues round new words and start to produce them comfortably

... **mechanically**, putting this new language into simple phrases and sentences.

To build security and confidence, students need to repeat words **safely**, without feeling inhibited by excess pressure from either the teacher or their peers. Drills should also be fun, lively, and varied. There are many ways to drill. It's best to learn and use as wide a range as you can.

1 Choral drills

The whole class repeats chorally after you, e.g.

T: *It's raining.*
Class: *It's raining.*

Where possible, try to add more meaning and fun by supplying a mime for students to copy as they say the words, e.g. wiggling your fingers in a downwards movement for raining, screwing up your face for *I didn't enjoy it*, pointing to your eyes for *I saw a film yesterday*, etc.

2 Individual drills

choral

individual

Individual students repeat when you indicate them and/or say their name, e.g.

T: *It's sunny. Juan?*
Juan: *It's sunny.*
T: *Marc?*
Marc: *It's sunny.*
T: *Sam?*
Sam: *It's sunny.*
T: *Everybody?*
Class: *It's sunny.*

A lively chorus can rouse a sleepy class, and provide a change of pace and focus. Mix individual and choral drills by saying *Everybody?* from time to time to ensure they're all listening, as above.

Both choral and individual drills work best when accompanied by a consistent gesture from you, so students know when to speak, e.g. beckoning with the digits of both hands for a whole class chorus, or pointing at individuals, as left.

It's important to drill at a good, brisk pace. With practice, you can drill even a large class quickly, especially if you avoid asking them to stand up each time before they speak, as my father had to when he was learning French!

Gesture

Consistent visual cues are essential for efficient drilling. Gestures with the hands, use of the eyes or a nod of the head both encourage and facilitate participation. They're also useful for guiding and improving pronunciation. Here are some ideas.

- 'Conduct' the class through a word using a beat for each syllable, highlighting the stress by raising your hand on the stressed syllable.

COM PU TER

- Count the number of syllables one at a time on the fingers of your raised hand and/or say *la-LA-la* for *computer*.

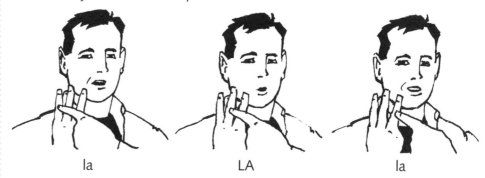

la LA la

- Mime punching yourself in the stomach for the SCHWA, as below.

/kəm/ /ˈpjuː/ /tə/

'Conducting' to accompany sentences, by raising your hands up or down to signal sentence stress and rises or falls is one of the few ways to drill intonation too.

Once students get used to these gestures, you can also use them for self-correction, e.g.

- To correct a student who makes a mistake during an individual drill, elicit the correct form from other students. This allows the person who made the mistake to hear and then say it correctly.
- For individual students who you hear making a mistake when monitoring pairwork, guide students towards the correct pronunciation by miming or la-la-la-ing the correct form for words they say wrongly.

Other 'formations'
For variety, students can repeat in different groupings:

… first the right half of the class and then the left

… all the boys and then all the girls to see who can say it the best

… in groups, columns or a row at a time.

This can be more fun if it's sometimes competitive between groups, to see which can say it the best.

If you intend to do a lot of drilling, want some extra variety and have time to do so, for fun you can divide them in more intricate ways, e.g.

… those whose first names begin with the letters A to M and then those from N to Z

… those whose birthdays are from January to June and then those from July to December, etc.

3 Silent drills

This might sound like a contradiction, but it's actually a very effective technique.

- Before you model the target phrase, say *Listen to me but don't say anything aloud. You have to repeat what I say silently to yourself five times. But I'm only going to say it once.*

- Give an example of mentally repeating a word five times. Cue the students with *Are you ready?* When they are silent, say it once. They repeat it to themselves silently.

- Then, elicit the word back from them to see who can say it best, or move onto repetition drilling, or repeat the procedure once more.

Some teachers tend to over-drill a phrase using just one technique, usually repeating aloud. Students process, learn and remember language equally well through silent repetition to themselves. It also saves your voice and the impact of a few moments of total silence can be quite powerful, as well as a relief!

4 'Almost silent' drills

Ask students to repeat words aloud five times quietly to themselves on a given signal. I use a raised open hand, so students see my five outstretched digits.

On this signal, students put their heads down, look at their knees (so they're concentrating and so it's easier to hear their own voices), and repeat the word five times quietly to themselves. It's fun and adds a bit more spark to drilling. Physically, it's also one of the few ways in which students can get near to actually hearing their own voices speaking English.

5 Back-chaining

No matter how expert you are, it's almost impossible to get large classes to chorus a long or difficult sentence together at exactly the same time and speed. It's much easier to get the correct rhythm, sentence stress, weak forms and intonation if you drill the sentence backwards, in chunks. It adds variety too. Here is an example of how to drill *He works in a large factory in London.*

T: *in London.* (Then say and/or gesture *Together.*)
Class: *in London.*
T: *in a large factory in London.* (Then gesture.)
Class: *in a large factory in London.*
T: *He works in a large factory in London.* (Then gesture.)
Class: *He works in a large factory in London.*
T: *Again.* (Then gesture.)
Class: *He works in a large factory in London.*

Note: Be careful how you choose the 'chunks' to avoid distorting the rhythm.

6 Mood drills

All drills, both those above and those which follow, benefit from an injection of humour if you sometimes model words in fun and silly ways. Use a chart like the one opposite or on PHOTOCOPIABLE PAGE 6, copying the moods expressed in the faces on it to model the words in different ways.

You can say them:
1 as slowly as you can 2 happily 3 sadly 4 angrily 5 as fast as you can
6 as loudly as you can 7 as quietly as you can, whispering
8 as if you were totally surprised 9 as well as you can, with a perfect English accent
10 with your teeth together 11 as badly as you can, with a terrible L1 accent
12 as if you were in love

Students copy the model in the given mood, e.g.

T: *Good afternoon.* (happily and pointing to the happy face) *Together.*
Class: *Good afternoon.* (quite happily)
T: *Come on! Again.*
Class: *Good afternoon.* (much more happily)
T: *OK! Good afternoon.* (very sadly and pointing to the sad face) *Together.*
Class: *Good afternoon!* (sadly)
T: *That's not very sad. Come on! Again.*
Class: *Good afternoon!* (said very sadly), etc.

Alternatively, point at a face, cue students with a gesture and ask them to say the new word or phrase according to the mood they see. Because the pictures are self-evident, they can see the manner in which they're supposed to speak so you don't need to provide a model each time, e.g.

T: *Good afternoon.* (say it normally, then point to the happy face) *Together.*
Class: *Good afternoon.* (very happily)
T: *Again.*
Class: *Good afternoon.* (very happily)
T: *Come on. Be happy! Again.*
Class: *Good afternoon!* (even more happily)
T: (points to sad face) *Together.*
Class: *Good afternoon!* (sadly)
T: *Again.*
Class: *Good afternoon!* (more sadly), etc.

With a bit of practice, you can take them right round the chart just by pointing and gesturing, asking them to repeat language many times without having to say a word yourself. Although this may seem mad, it works, especially with younger secondary students. Even those in their mid-teens are more likely to pay attention and respond if they're encouraged to respond in different, amusing ways from time to time. The chart can also be used for pairwork. ◆ SEE PAGE 54

7 Substitution drills

Ask students to change one or two words in the phrase as it will be more meaningful than just repeating it, e.g.

T:	*I'm going to a party tonight. Together.*
Class:	*I'm going to a party tonight.*
T:	*The cinema. Andrea.*
Andrea:	*I'm going to the cinema tonight.*
T:	*Good. A restaurant. Tomas.*
Tomas:	*I'm going to a restaurant tonight,* etc.

This can become more fun if from time to time you respond naturally to what you've made them say, e.g.

T:	*The cinema. Andrea.*
Andrea:	*I'm going to the cinema tonight.*
T:	*Really? What film are you going to see?*
Andrea:	*Er, James Bond.*
T:	*Oh yuk! Right. A restaurant. Tomas,* etc.

Simple one or two word substitution drills like this work well to practise with the whole class. However, it's best to avoid putting students on the spot by asking them to make more complex transformations instantly, with all the class listening.

8 Open pairs

For basic question/answer exchanges a good way to practise is in pairs selected randomly by you across the class, not in closed groups. This is called OPEN PAIRS.

Once an exchange has been established, elect a student to play each role, e.g. *Marisa, ask the question. Elena, answer.* This leads to:

Marisa: *Where are you from, Elena?*
Elena: *I'm from (Lerida).*

The rest of the class listens. You could say two more names for them to do the same thing or, alternatively, ask Elena to ask the question and nominate who should answer, e.g.

Elena: *Where are you from, Xavier?*

This technique provides more variety and also has a number of advantages.

- Students get used to speaking together with you still in control, so you can work on getting it right while you've got everyone's attention.
- Modelling the exchange and behaviour required ensures everybody knows what to do before they do it together in CLOSED PAIRS.
- You can make students who wouldn't normally talk to each other do so.
- Provided you've done enough basic drilling, you can make students who don't normally volunteer language get used to speaking in front of the class with relative security, because they should be able to get it right.
- If they know you're likely to do this, students will be more attentive in case they're suddenly going to be put on the spot.
- The words carry more meaning when students are asking and answering together.
- The class can enjoy the freedom of choosing who answers the next question, and begin to personalise their practice.

Which of the drills above did your language teacher use at school? Which of these didn't you enjoy? Which of the others would you have enjoyed?

CHAPTER 7

Repetition drills in pairs and groups

The quicker you can get to pairwork, the more efficient and more personal drills can become. Students in CLOSED PAIRS and groups can practise together much more economically in terms of class time. It also saves your voice and is a more effective way for you to monitor individual progress, as well as being much more fun for your students.

Below, we look at four basic practice techniques to encourage students to drill and help each other together in pairs and groups.

1 Reading aloud
2 Using coursebook dialogues
3 Question/answer drills from pictures
4 Question/answer drills from written prompts

Before you read, answer this question: Do you use the above techniques with students in pairs and you listening? Why (not)? Which one works best?

1 Reading aloud

And so we return to my French class experience (SEE PAGE 5)! Reading aloud is a specific, difficult skill. It involves:

… looking at text
… recognising words and remembering how to say them correctly
… hopefully having time to understand what it means
… saying it correctly and trying to inject some life into the words.

This is totally different from how we usually perform these skills. We usually read in silence, at our own speed and faster than we would say the words, and we usually speak to other people who don't have a script of what we're going to say and so have to listen. In other words, it doesn't really practise either skill, particularly if the text is a narrative.

It's also difficult to concentrate on the meaning and since it involves doing several things at once, many of us make mistakes, even in L1 and especially in a foreign language. Apart from actors, the only time most of us read aloud is:

… reading something aloud from a notice or newspaper to a friend
… reading a story to a child
… in public-speaking (e.g. at a wedding or funeral), which is nerve-wracking.

It's only really useful for pronunciation practice of spoken texts, e.g. dialogues. Then it can help to coach students in aspects of connected speech, making it more comprehensible through work on word-linking, sentence stress, weak forms, etc. before moving on to ROLEPLAYING. Here are some suggestions.

- Make sure students have had sufficient opportunity to listen to the dialogue before being asked to read it aloud. It's more efficient to read the text aloud yourself than force them to do it.

- Highlight potential problems like stress and weak forms and drill words you know they will have problems with. It's useful to take students through a text first, helping them to underline the syllables to stress, highlight the SCHWA sounds, etc.

- Then ask students to read it together in pairs and groups rather than to the rest of the class so all of them are much more actively involved. If they've heard it enough times, they're more likely to be able to help each other and ask you when they're not sure without slowing everybody else down.

In addition, reading aloud can be adapted and greatly improved using some of the techniques suggested below. ◆ SEE PHOTOCOPIABLE PAGE 11 AND PAGE 65

2 Using coursebook dialogues

These are perhaps the most common source of spoken language in coursebooks and teachers are always looking for ways to get beyond reading aloud, gap-filling, comprehension, true/false or multiple-choice questions. Before you read on, stop and think about how else you can deal with dialogues.

Insist students never speak without making eye contact

Making and maintaining eye contact is very important in 'real life'. Even if they're only reading aloud in pairs, force them to look at the page, remember their line(s), then look up and speak to their partner, not just speak to the book.

This simple technique makes a world of difference: the words begin to assume some meaning and feel more real, and it's much easier to imagine the context.

Remember dialogues from prompts

Rather than just reading the lines, it's much more satisfactory if students are asked to remember part or all of them from prompts. This is easily done in a number of ways.

Skeleton prompts

- Put SKELETON PROMPTS from any dialogue on the board, using the (/) to represent missing word(s):

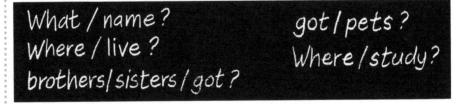

What / name?
Where / live?
brothers / sisters / got?

got / pets?
Where / study?

- If you do this for the questions only as above, ask the student who's answering to look away from the board or cover their eyes so they can't see the prompts and have to listen. You can organise this by having pairs face each other, but with one facing the board and the other facing away.
- Then, when they swap roles, ask the second student to ask the questions in a different order so their partner really has to listen.
- If you do this for both the questions and answers, make sure students look at each other when they speak and not at the board.

Key words and pictures

The same can be done with coursebook dialogues in the margin of the coursebook itself, either with pictures or words.

- Students look at any dialogue and have to choose two key words to help them to remember each line.

- Then they write them in the margin to the left of the speakers' names. Or they can draw pictures, or a mixture of both, as below.

morning / help	Shop assistant:	*Good morning. Can I help you?*
🍎🍏	Customer:	*I'd like a kilo of apples, please.*
which?	Shop assistant:	*Yes, madam. Which ones would you like?*
green?	Customer:	*How much are those green ones?*
(50p)(10p)	Shop assistant:	*They're 60p a kilo.*
red?	Customer:	*And those red ones over there?*
🇺🇸 / (50p)(20p)(10p)(5p)	Shop assistant:	*They're American. They're 85p a kilo.*
green / 🍌 ?	Customer:	*I'll have the green ones. And have you got any bananas?*

- Limiting them to two words means they have to choose carefully. This involves mentally processing the lines several times and really thinking about the language, its meaning and which are the key words. The option to draw also makes them think about which words they can represent easily.

- When they're ready, students cover all the dialogue, e.g. with their notebooks or a piece of paper. They look only at their prompts and the speakers' names.

- In pairs, they look only at the prompts and remember and say their lines without looking at the dialogue.

- If they can't remember something, they can always lift the 'cover', look quickly under the paper and then carry on. Ask students to count how many times they have to look and award a prize to the pair who remember best!

These prompts are good ways of training students, to help them to memorise language at home. ◆ SEE PAGE 74

Disappearing dialogue

- Copy onto the board any coursebook dialogue, or an invented one, e.g.

  A: *What are you doing after school today?*
  B: *I'm going to the beach for a game of football. How about you?*
  A: *Nothing special. Can I go with you?*
  B: *Sure. We're going by bus. We're meeting at the bus-stop.*
  A: *OK, great. See you there.*
  B: *Right, but don't be late! I'm not waiting for you again.*

- Students practise in pairs. Then erase a few words, replacing each one with a line to indicate that something is missing. By choosing carefully which words you rub out, you can focus specifically on verb forms, auxiliaries, articles, adjectives, etc. or just keep it general, e.g.

  A: *What _____ you doing after _____ today?*
  B: *I _____ going to _____ beach for _____ game of football. _____ about you?*
  A: *Nothing _____ . Can I _____ with you?*
  B: *Sure. We're _____ by bus. We're meeting at _____ bus-stop.*
  A: *OK, _____ . See you _____ .*
  B: *Right, _____ don't be late! I'm not waiting _____ you again.*

● Students swap roles and do it again, perhaps using a different mood as suggested in the last chapter. Then erase a few more words. Try to leave a few key words each time so they can make some sense of it, e.g.

A: What _____ you _____ after _____ today?
B: _____ _____ going to _____ beach for _____ game _____ football. _____ about you?
A: Nothing _____ . _____ I _____ with _____ ?, etc.

● If you're feeling really sadistic, you can reduce it further or ask them to do it without any help whatsoever! This is a handy technique, so don't overdo it by taking it too far or using it too often!

Another alternative is to cue some words with either their first letter, first two or three letters or half the words, rather than erase them all, e.g.

A: Wh_____ a_____ you do_____ after sch_____ today?
B: I'm go_____ to the b_____ for a g_____ of foo_____ . _____ about you?
A: Nothing sp_____ . C_____ I g_____ wi_____ you?, etc.

Again it's best to mix and vary the way you do this to retain interest.

Storyboarding

A technique which is popular now in computer programmes is STORYBOARDING. For a short dialogue revising known language, it works equally well on the board. Although not really a drill, it's a very useful dialogue/speaking technique.

● Write a skeleton dialogue on the board, using a line for each missing word, giving students all punctuation and any proper nouns, e.g.

A: _____ _____ _____ _____ _____ _____ , Paolo?
B: _____ , _____ _____ _____ _____ Suzanna.

● Tell the class the context, e.g. it's two students talking. They have to guess the missing words. They get a point for each one they guess. Play this in two or three teams, e.g. half the class against the other.

● Students take turns to guess. If they guess correctly, write the word in the dialogue, give them a point and tell them to have another go. If they guess wrongly, the next team guesses, and so on until they get it all.

● If they find it hard or get stuck, give extra clues, e.g. the first or last letters, the number of letters and/or a grammatical clue (It's a noun, It rhymes with 'pool', It's a popular sport, It's a verb, etc.). You might reach this stage:

A: Are you d_ _ _ _ a_ _ _ _ _ _ _ g after _ _ _ oo _ , Paolo?
B: Yes, I'm _ _ ing c _ c _ ing with Suzanna.

When they've finally guessed it, students can then practise the dialogue in pairs using any of the ideas above.

3 Question/answer drills from pictures

This can just be questions from pictures or objects in the classroom, e.g.
A: What's this in English?
B: It's a crash helmet. What's this?, etc.

Alternatively, use questions about FLASHCARDS stuck on the board, e.g.

Nick   Liam and Noel   Madonna   Eddy   Sue

BLU-TACK the pictures on the board, number them 1 to 4 or elicit and write some names under them as above. Once students know the language, put them in pairs to practise. They're an incredibly flexible resource for any tense.

A: *What does Nick like doing?*   or   A: *What does Nick do at the weekends?*
B: *He likes swimming.*   B: *He goes swimming.*

or

A: *What did Nick do yesterday?*   or   A: *What's Nick doing this afternoon?*
B: *He went swimming.*   B: *He's going swimming.*

The possibilities are endless and students can speak easily and comfortably in pairs, without the need for translation. You can make it more meaningful by having one student turn his/her back, cover or close his/her eyes and try to answer the questions from memory, then swap roles.

4 Question/answer drills from other written prompts

These can be skeleton or single word prompts on the board or on paper. For example, when teaching beginners, I always have a lot of pieces of paper with word prompts like this:

Name
Phone number
From
Address

At any point in one lesson or to revise in the next, I can give them to students to ask and answer in pairs, e.g. *What's your name?/What's your phone number?*, etc. One student has the paper, the other listens and answers, then they swap roles, asking and answering in a different order. They can sometimes write in the answers, as if filling in a simple form, but the main aim is to get them speaking.

They're incredibly simple to produce, very effective, and define each time to students what they're supposed to know and be able to say. After we've learned a few more exchanges, I add them onto a longer prompt sheet:

First name	*From*
Surname	*Address*
Phone number	*Who/live with*
Dialling code	*Hobbies*

I always keep a few sets with my register for emergencies, fillers, etc. You can always do this on the board with one student turning away and answering, then swapping roles and asking in a different order. Or you can quickly rewrite the prompts on the board in a different order the second time. ◆ SEE *SPLASH*, PAGE 57

Make a list of twelve word prompts for questions one of your classes should know. Copy the list as many times as you can onto a single sheet of paper. Photocopy if necessary so you have a list per pair in your class, then cut it into strips using a guillotine. Next lesson, quickly revise the questions with the whole class, then try it in CLOSED PAIRS.

CHAPTER 8

Pair and groupwork that works

For teachers either unsure of what pair and groupwork are or who remain unconvinced of their worth, this brief introduction answers some of their questions. It's followed on page 44 by detailed guidelines to show how to introduce and make them work in class.

"What is pairwork?" It is when you divide a class into pairs of students. Each pair practises speaking together simultaneously to each other, not to the teacher.

"What is groupwork?" The same thing as pairwork, only with students working in groups. A group can be anything from three students to half the class or more. Pairwork is good preparation for groupwork, although generally with adolescents, the smaller the group, the easier it is for them to maintain self-control. Once you get beyond three or four, it's very hard for students to concentrate and keep speaking English for very long unless you're playing a team game.

"Why use pair and groupwork?"
- It greatly increases the amount of time students can talk in class, especially in larger classes. In fact, it's the best way to maximise class time.
- It also improves the quality of talking, allowing for more of the features of natural speech: hesitation, mixed structures, unfinished sentences, etc.
- If language is viewed as an interactive tool, then it should be taught interactively. Speaking is an active process rarely carried out in isolation, so it's a natural framework for interaction, i.e. talking to somebody as in real life.
- It encourages a more communal classroom atmosphere and helps to individualise language learning and teaching. Changing groupings enables a variety of learning experiences for students. They can learn from each other and teachers are freer to help individuals, thus producing a better affective classroom climate.
- If you believe, as I do, that students learn by doing things for themselves, then this provides an opportunity for them to do so. Above all, it's more motivating for students and teachers once they're used to it, which doesn't take long.

Compare this with the 'traditional' alternative, i.e. with the teacher at the front and the class as an audience who sit, receive, listen and then respond.

Traditional teaching	Pair/groupwork
The teacher initiates any exchange.	Students initiate their own exchanges.
One student, usually selected by the teacher, responds to the teacher.	Other students respond together.
The teacher judges the acceptability of the response (usually on grounds of grammatical/phonological ACCURACY).	Students judge the acceptability of their words more naturally, i.e. whether other students have 'got the message', as in real life.
The focus is nearly always on ACCURACY.	The focus is mainly on FLUENCY, though can include ACCURACY, depending on the activity.

Traditional teaching	Pair/groupwork
The rest of the class listen but don't have to do anything.	Students listen to each other more willingly as they're more likely to have to respond.
All go at the same speed, dictated by the teacher.	There is more variety as students talk at once. They can more easily go at their own speed.
Performing publicly in front of all their peers at once creates pressure.	Performing in front of far fewer peers and at a lower volume is more private.
Much of the teacher's time is spent leading the class, selecting who will speak and judging each individual's performance.	The teacher is freer to listen to more students at once. They'll be speaking in a more relaxed and natural environment. The teacher can offer more individual help.
There is little opportunity for students to say what they want to, or contribute more freely.	Students have space to be able to express their own personalities.

- If the teacher leads every exchange and talks only to students individually, in a 40-minute class with a class of 40 students, the maximum each student can speak is a minute at most (and this is unlikely, given teacher-talking time). Two five-minute pairwork activities in the same lesson increase this to five minutes for each and every student, i.e. five times more practice.

- Classroom dynamics and atmosphere improve dramatically if students are asked to work together in situations where, in other school subjects, they would normally be expected to work alone, e.g. writing answers to exercises. However, groupwork is now becoming a more common practice in many other school subjects too, especially where project work is being introduced.

- When teaching oral English, your long-term aim should be for students to talk more than you in class. That obviously can't happen overnight. It requires methodical, step-by-step training and regular practice. If students are to get enough practice in class, it also requires pair and groupwork.

"OK, but it's more work for me. Are there any other advantages?"

Compared with traditional methods, it makes classes much more active and enjoyable for students, so it's more likely to motivate them to want to learn. But is it really harder for you? In terms of preparation, once you've learned a range of techniques and built up a bank of activities, pictures, rolecards, etc. it ultimately saves time and can make life much easier.

In class, instead of doing most of the talking, constantly having to lead and control everything your class does, you have more opportunity to listen to your class to see how they're progressing, to respond to them as individuals and establish a different, more adult relationship with them.

"But it's harder for my students too."

On the contrary, once they've got used to it, it can give them more confidence. Students feel infinitely more secure talking quietly to somebody next to them, than individually with the pressure of the whole class listening to them speaking a foreign language.

It's also a way of treating students with respect and encouraging them to work more autonomously. They can help each other, which aids maturity and makes them less dependent on us.

"When can I use pair and groupwork?"

Since both are language practice vehicles, the answer is almost always, whenever you want students to use each other to practise and/or share what they know. You first need to present and drill language until students are able to try to say it on their own. After this, however, pairwork can be used at almost **any** time in any lesson. Indeed it is only **in**appropriate when working with a partner might upset concentration or when you really want students to work or respond individually.

Pairwork activities are usually easier to set up, manage and control than groupwork, so it's a good idea to get students used to speaking in pairs before moving onto groupwork. Once they're used to both, activities which begin in pairs can often move into groups, e.g. to compare results.

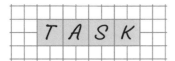

Look at the practice activities in any unit of your coursebook. Which do you think are most suitable for pairwork and which for groupwork? Mark them PW or GW. Then look in the accompanying teacher's book to see what is suggested.

Making pairwork work: a step-by-step overview

1 Choose easy-to-manage activities first

Don't ask students to run before they can walk! If they've never done pair or groupwork before, a complicated INFORMATION-GAP activity or ROLEPLAY may be a disaster! Start with short, simple activities and progress from there. An effective starting point is a two-minute pairwork question/answer drill prompted by:

… pictures on the board or from the coursebook (SEE PAGE 27)

… prompts after a dialogue-building activity (SEE PAGE 28) or on pieces of paper (SEE PAGE 41)

… the everyday activities suggested in CHAPTER 9.

2 Make sure students have got the language that they need

For any activity, try to predict the words that students will need, especially at very low levels. Quickly rehearse the activity yourself as if you were a student. Ask yourself: *Do my students know the words I'm using? Can they express what they'll need to say?* As ever, there will always be unforeseen language, but make sure you've taught most or all of the language that you know they'll need.

Equally important is that students know what to do if they want to say things in English that you haven't taught. Do they:

… use L1?   … have access to a bilingual dictionary to find new words?

… ask you?   … say nothing and give up?

… ask other students?   … start talking about what they're doing after school? etc.

At least students should know that it's acceptable to use L1 to say things that they can't express in English.

3 Choose the most appropriate grouping.

Pair or groupwork?

This choice obviously depends on the activity, e.g. a simple question/answer exchange is usually better in pairs, whereas a guessing game like *Twenty questions* (SEE PAGE 66), which requires imagination and a lot of language, works better in groups.

Basically, if you want to maximise student talking time, pairwork is the most efficient means. It's also a more feasible vehicle for ACCURACY practice and for the students to try to work in English. However, groupwork can be more enjoyable, especially for games, activities in teams and larger tasks such as PROJECTS. Weaker students can sometimes find more support in groups but they can also 'hide' and more easily avoid having to say anything. The optimum grouping is often suggested in the teacher's book for commercial materials. Usually the decision is straightforward but there's no harm in experimenting. Remember too that you can always begin in pairs, and then combine these pairs into larger groups to compare notes.

Composition of groups

Whether to mix levels of ability or group stronger and weaker students separately is more difficult to decide. The aim should be to:

… avoid stronger students dominating the class or pulling it along too quickly

… find ways to encourage stronger students to work with and help the weaker ones so they can catch up.

If the stronger students always work together, it can stretch and motivate them but the weaker ones will never have the chance to improve, so the imbalance increases. This necessitates:

… mixing the levels of ability within pairs and groups

… changing partners regularly to keep a balance/group dynamic.

Because of illness, changing friendships over the year, etc. both of these tend to happen naturally, but you should encourage it as much as possible.

Students often want to stay with the same partner all the time and sometimes, provided they're happy and not disruptive, it's easier just to let them. Forcing groupings, especially on students who don't get on, can work against you. However, if you do several pairwork activities in the same lesson, a change of partner provides more variety. Move only one student from one side of the class to the other, then everybody just turns their head and works with the student on the other side of them.

What to do if you have an odd number of students

Here are some ideas.

- Work with the extra student yourself, especially in a small class. Make sure the other pairs or groups are all under way, then play one of the roles yourself. You can usually finish the activity more quickly, leaving you free to monitor the rest of the class a little. This can sometimes be useful as you can choose which student to help, e.g. a particularly weak, ill-disciplined or strong one. It's useful for you to work individually with students from time to time, anyway.

- Give two students one role to share, i.e. have two As and one B, or two Bs and one A, whichever role is more appropriate. Avoid always choosing the same student to share roles.

- Make the extra student a monitor or 'secretary', who has to listen to other groups, help to look up words they don't know in the dictionary or note and correct mistakes, or even help you to control the amount of L1 they use.

4 Choose the best available classroom layout

Arrange the classroom to suit the interaction pattern. Your aim should be to:

… maximise opportunities for students to talk comfortably

… make sure everybody gets a chance to speak

… move around the class yourself, get near enough to hear them all, monitor, help and correct them as necessary.

Students should be speaking face to face. It's more natural, enjoyable and much easier. They have to look at each other, otherwise the words carry no meaning.

If you can't move your furniture, there's always something you can do, e.g.

… students can always turn their heads to face the student(s) next to, behind or in front of them

… they can stand and face each other

… one of the pair (or two of the group) can stand while the other(s) sits

… others can stand in groups at the front of the class, etc.

Most classrooms allow more space at the front of the class than the teacher needs and this can be shared from time to time with students.

Physically moving prevents boredom, providing a useful change of focus. Make sure you decide your preferred formations for each stage of the lesson beforehand. With a bit of practice students can easily be trained to make the changes from one formation to another smoothly. ◆ SEE PAGE 48

5 Be sure of your aims and give clear instructions

To set up activities, clear instructions are crucial. Here are some ways to do this.

Use L1 to give and clarify instructions

Use L1 if necessary, especially with a low-level group doing any complex activity. Given that you only have about 40 minutes in which to teach anything, a two-minute explanation of an activity which then produces a lot of student talk is clear, economical and avoids all sorts of misunderstandings.

Use both L1 and English

Give the instructions two or three times in clear, simple English. Then ask students to explain in their L1 what they've understood and exactly what they have to do before they then do the activity in English.

Alternatively, use L1 to explain:

… the language aims, e.g. *This is to practise making questions and answers.*

… the context, e.g. *You're in a shop. You want to buy some chewing gum.*

… the communicative objective, e.g. *You have to buy three things but you've only got £5.00 to spend.*

Then give the same explanation in English so students get used to hearing English instructions. Eventually, you'll be able to do most of it in English.

Show them several times

Whether you use English or L1 to explain an activity, it's almost always essential to demonstrate physically what's going to happen. Look at this example of a ROLEPLAY about going shopping.

● Play the more difficult role yourself first (e.g. the shop assistant). Give the other role to a student who you think will be able to cope, usually one of the stronger students. Do this with several students if you think it's necessary.

● When you finish, swap roles. You play the customer with the same student, a different student or the class taking turns to ask the shop assistant's questions.

- If you think it's necessary to demonstrate further, nominate two students to do it again, with the rest of the class and you helping them as necessary. They can do this most easily from their seats (OPEN PAIRS) or by coming out and performing in front of the class (if you're confident they can do it).
- Only when you're sure all the students know what to do should you finally attempt to move into pairwork (CLOSED PAIRS), to do the same.
- Above all, make sure they know how to start and who's going to speak first. If necessary, put the first lines they have to say on the board. Once you have got them started they're usually able to keep going, so make sure they know exactly how to begin.

Note: No matter how clear your instructions, most monolingual students will confirm together in L1 what they have to do. This is perfectly natural; it reassures them that they've understood before trying to speak English together.

6 Make sure students know the focus and aim, and give a time limit

Always tell the students the answers to the following five questions.

1 Is it an ACCURACY or FLUENCY activity?

2 Should they be speaking and listening only, or should they be writing too, or correcting any mistakes their partner makes?

3 What do they do if they can't say something? Do they use L1 and not worry, ask you at once, use a dictionary, note the words or expressions they need and ask you later?

4 How long have they got? (It's much easier for students to 'play the game' and talk together if they know they've only got to do it for two minutes.)

5 How will they know when they've finished? What do they do then?

7 Make sure students listen to the answers in pairwork

As with any other pairwork activity, what's crucial is for the questioner to listen to the answer, not just ask all the questions without thinking, which is not very interesting. Here are some ways to ensure this.

Always ask follow-up questions if possible

If students ask and answer only the questions on the page, it's just an interrogation. No real conversation is taking place. If you insist they ask another question each time, they obviously have to choose an appropriate one and so listen to their partner.

Generally, with question/answer type drills and pairwork speaking activities, try to get students into the habit of always asking FOLLOW-UP QUESTIONS in English whenever their partner responds to a question, not just ignoring the answer. In other words, they should try to ask another question or even two when appropriate, even if only *What about you?* This is the main advance students should make as they progress from beginner to elementary levels.

Insist they summarise what they've heard

Here are some suggestions.

- The interviewer remembers and repeats the information received to his/her partner, who corrects any misunderstandings if necessary.
- Alternatively, they could swap partners and tell a third student what they have learned about their first partner.
- Another idea is for them each to tell you one or two interesting things they have learned about their partner.

The students can also do any of the above in writing.

Other ways to make sure they're listening

- Don't let the listener see any prompts; he/she should look only at his/her partner's face.
- Monitor them yourself and ask questions to the interviewers as they go along to see what they can remember.
- Make sure they ask the questions in a different order when they swap roles.

All the above ideas are essentially ways of creating an INFORMATION GAP. ◆ SEE PAGE 62 They are crucial too for the FLUENCY activities in CHAPTER 12.

Think of a pairwork activity which you've used recently. Which extra ingredient from the above could you add to make students listen to each other better?

8 Make activities easy to manage

Students can be trained to help you run the lesson quietly and quickly.

Learn to start and stop activities

Have an efficient system for stopping/starting groupwork, e.g. a raised hand signal from you which signifies that they should all raise their own hands and stop talking at once. A fun way to encourage students to co-operate is to tell them that the record achieved by your previous class was total silence and all hands up in five seconds. Ask them if they can beat it!

Don't go on too long

It's much better to stop activities at their peak before they peter out, the lesson loses pace and your students lose interest. Several short, simple activities provide a much more varied and enjoyable lesson than one overlong or complex one.

Have an idea what you're going to do with groups who finish first

Try to have something prepared for fast finishers, or at least know what you're going to do with them. For example, they can:

... swap roles
... ask the questions again in a different order
... do it again, only better (e.g. with improved pronunciation and no mistakes)
... invent more examples of their own
... write a sentence or two
... just relax.

Always emphasise that in speaking activities the pair which finishes last have had the most practice!

Know what to do if things go wrong

The most common reasons for failure with pairwork are:

... not explaining and demonstrating an activity enough before asking students to do it alone
... not anticipating/pre-teaching enough of the necessary language
... choosing an activity which is too unusual/complicated compared to what the class is used to.

Note: If you see that an activity isn't working or hear several students all making the same mistake, don't think twice about calling a halt to repair the damage, before starting again! Be flexible, even after you've started an activity, e.g.

… explain it again in L1 and demonstrate the activity in L1 if necessary

… have a 'correction slot' to teach the words that they haven't understood or haven't been saying in English, before starting again

… write up some extra prompts on the board to help them, e.g. give SKELETON PROMPTS to help students to formulate phrases ◆ SEE PAGE 38

… abandon the activity altogether if you can't see how to make it work easily.

9 Monitor activities so you appear to be listening to all of them

Once you've asked students to work together, if you just sit at your desk and appear uninterested, it's unlikely that they'll speak English for long. This is especially true for those seated further away from you towards the back of the class. You should at least appear to be listening to all of them. This doesn't mean running round the classroom, squeezing between desks like a headless chicken!

Scan the class with your eyes

Students can then see you watching them. A smile to encourage, a glare to control, a laugh from you when they start laughing, all make the students think that you're listening and want them to perform well.

Scan the class with your ears

It's surprisingly easy to pick up on those who are using L1 rather than English. Even in large classes you can still hear quite a lot of errors. Whether you're writing on the board or filling in the register, your ears can still monitor and you should react appropriately to what you hear.

Move nearer to the students

Sitting on your desk or standing in front of it, rather than behind it makes you much more accessible to students and physically shows them that there's a change of focus. Ideally, you should either move right around the class at least once so you can speak to and help everybody, or try to get into the middle of the class where you can hear and be near the largest number of students at once. To avoid intimidating them too much, either sit or squat down low so you do not overshadow any particular student or group, as left.

By turning your head from side to side you can at least appear to be watching and listening to all the groups at once. Make eye contact with individual students, perhaps to smile and encourage or frown if they break into L1. From this central position, you can:

… quickly move to help, correct or control problem groups as necessary

… specifically choose to monitor/be near those students who you know will either cause or have the most problems, i.e. troublemakers or weaker students.

It's important to be aware of the effect of your physical presence. The nearer you are to students the more intimidated they can become. Sometimes this can be a useful control device, but if you tower over students rather than keeping a discreet distance or squatting down a bit, you can really unsettle them.

Use the students to help you monitor

For example, tell students to ask you for help if they need it, rather than switch to L1 or simply stop. Another way of monitoring is to elect a group 'monitor' or 'secretary' to note any key errors or ideas that they couldn't express.

10 Know how you're going to correct

A lot of classroom correction has to be improvised as unpredicted errors arise. But you should know your aims and whether you're going to ignore errors, deal with the main ones or sometimes even try to correct all of them.

How, when, and how much you correct will depend on the type of activity, your aims (ACCURACY or FLUENCY) and the time available. If you do run out of time, you can always begin the next lesson by putting six sentences containing the mistakes on the board as a warmer, for students to correct.

Here are a few points to remember.

- A lot of quick oral correction can be done as you monitor. Either quickly tell the student their mistake or elicit the error by repeating the wrong phrase for them to try to correct themselves.

- Don't forget to use all the available resources, e.g. refer students to the grammar reviews in their coursebooks, a bilingual dictionary, etc.

- In groupwork, it's easier to note any recurring errors and deal with them once the activity has finished.

- A useful pairwork technique is to train students to note down in L1 anything important that they wanted to say but couldn't and then carry on to the end of the activity, rather than calling on you to help them. Once the activity is over, you can then deal with these problems and explain to the whole class at once. This is much more economical and gives you considerably more time.

- With a smaller class, you can write the correct version of phrases they've misused on strips of paper and give them to students to read while or after they speak. This provides a more concrete record for them.

- Announcing to the whole class *Sophie made this mistake* and asking them to correct it for her is a sure way to demotivate and embarrass her. A much friendlier way to show Sophie her mistake is either to say it or write it anonymously on the board, saying *Some of you made this mistake. What should it be?* and elicit the answer without pressure on any individual(s).

Overcorrection can demotivate and make students reluctant to try again. It stifles FLUENCY, so choose only key points. Some teachers are overkeen to find the 'right' answer quickly and to move on. Exploring mistakes in a positive way can make students feel less uncomfortable about making them. Ultimately, you won't be able to correct every single mistake anyway, nor should you aspire to!

11 Don't forget to provide feedback

Always provide feedback to the class as a whole, however minimal. Praise and encourage regularly to try to make students' learning a positive experience and highlight what they've achieved, e.g. say *Well done. That was good. Your English is getting better. You did it without speaking L1 – thank you! Thank you for speaking quietly*, etc. Feedback can usefully focus on areas that are later going to be evaluated, e.g. *What's the past tense of (X)?*

Equally important is to respond to students as individuals sometimes, even with larger classes. Over a term make sure you've spoken to everybody face to face in English just to make them feel that you care about their progress. Ideally, you would build in some kind of regular counselling to spend five minutes with each student to review their progress and feelings. ◆ SEE CHAPTER 14

T A S K

Think back to the last pair or groupwork activity that you did, or a recent one that didn't go too well. Which of the eleven points and sub-steps above could you have done better? Highlight them to help you to remember them.

CHAPTER 9

Everyday activities to familiarise students with pair and groupwork

The best way to help students to lose any feelings of self-consciousness and become comfortable speaking English together is to use pair and groupwork as often as possible. It's the most efficient way to maximise the opportunities for them to speak English.

Pair and groupwork can be used at almost **any** time in **any** lesson and for homework as well. On average, the students in my classes are always either in pairs or groups for well over half the lesson. I bumped into an old student of mine recently, and the first thing she remembered about my classes was *two – two – two – two – two – two* and the 'scissors' mime with two fingers, which are the instruction and gesture I give to put them in pairs.

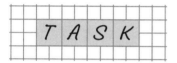

Can you think of two or three activities which you do in class where pair or groupwork is inappropriate?

It is only inappropriate when working with a partner might upset concentration, i.e. when we're presenting new language, drilling, or formally testing individuals, or when students are reading or listening. Most other things which students do in class can be done at least as well and usually better together rather than alone. I honestly can't think of a lesson when I haven't used pair or groupwork at some point, apart from classes devoted to formal tests.

Here are some simple activities which you can use nearly every day.

1 Do it together, not alone

Many classroom activities traditionally performed between the teacher and a single student can either be done entirely in pairs/small groups, or have a group stage added to them, for students to speak more. Here are some examples.

Discussing questions together

- When answering your questions, e.g. for reading or listening comprehension, ask the question as usual but instead of asking one individual to tell you the answer straight away, make all students tell their partner what they think the answer is. That way everybody gets a chance to answer. Students also tend to repeat your question between them, which is useful. Weaker students have the added support of a partner to help them to formulate an answer and tell them what the question means if necessary. Having someone else give 'their' answer can boost confidence too. Then elicit the answer from a pair or two. Naturally, it takes longer to get through the questions, but students become much more involved in the answers.

- This also works well for activities like *Spot the mistake*. Put five sentences on the board, each containing a mistake, perhaps from homework or that you've heard in a speaking activity. In pairs, students have to spot the mistakes together, orally agree what the correct version is, then tell you.

- After doing any written exercise alone, students can compare and check their answers together before the teacher confirms with the whole class. Much of what they say will be in L1 unless you're prepared to monitor furiously, but that doesn't matter. The focus is on English words and they at least have to vocalise those that they chose for their answers.

Writing together

Students can do **any** written exercise together in pairs/small groups rather than alone, e.g. grammar exercises, answering comprehension questions, even tests. In fact, if they can only see one copy of the test between them, this will encourage collaboration. The only difference is that they make more noise but it needn't be excessive, especially if you offer them the choice of doing it together if they co-operate with low volume, or alone if they can't.

Doing homework together

Students can do homework activities together in pairs/groups. Teachers often discourage this for fear of 'cheating', weaker students simply copying from the strong, etc. However, I find it a great way to get mixed-ability students to help each other. The focus is on English, the product is in English and students inevitably have to vocalise at least some of the words as they work together, thus speaking more. ◆ SEE CHAPTER 13

2 Brainstorm together

Revising vocabulary

Before a test (or for general vocabulary revision) give students in pairs/small groups a time limit, e.g. three minutes, to remember and produce a list of all the words they can from a known word group, e.g. classroom objects, family, irregular past participles, etc.

Elicit all their words onto the board to build a single class list. This is a good way to involve stronger and weaker students together in the same activity and expand vocabulary in a structured way.

Predicting answers

Before a gap-fill type activity (e.g. a dialogue, song or reading comprehension) ask students to read the text together and predict some of the answers, before they listen. This gives stronger students an opportunity to help the weaker ones.

Predicting vocabulary

Before a reading with a clear topic, students can BRAINSTORM a given number of words or phrases they expect to find, e.g. if the title were *Elephants*, students might come up with *big ears, grey, heavy, four feet* and *Africa*. The same applies to any listening with a clear topic or setting. Students can also BRAINSTORM phrases, e.g. in a shop dialogue *Can I help you? How much?*

In all three activities above students will come up with several words or phrases in L1 that they want to say but don't know or can't remember. This is an ideal time for you to introduce them. Insist that they ask you in English *How do you say (X) in English, please?* If it's a word you really think they ought to remember and are sure somebody else will know, get them to ask the rest of the class.

3 Remember together

Vocabulary

After you've presented a group of new words from a picture in the coursebook, tell students to close their books, and working in pairs or threes, to list (orally and/or in writing) all the items they can remember. Once they've remembered all they can, put two groups together for them to compare and combine their lists. Again, stronger students can help the weaker ones and this is as effective as any other language drill.

The best thing is that it gives students a clear, simple language practice task which doesn't involve you, leaving you free either to monitor and help with pronunciation or mentally prepare what you want to do next. It can also work well if you introduce an element of competition between the groups (*Which group can remember the most?*) and/or set them a time limit to race against (*Which group can remember the most words in two minutes?*).

Dialogues

Equally, after a dialogue which they've heard several times, students can try to reconstruct it from memory together. Put some SKELETON PROMPTS on the board to help them. ◆ SEE DIALOGUE-BUILDING, PAGE 28

Stories

After any story which they've read and had time to digest, students can close their books and retell it to a partner. A tells it to B then B tells it back to A. As ever, this works best if the listener has a task to make him or her listen and not just go to sleep while their partner talks, e.g. B can:

… prompt anything that A forgets as A speaks

… tell A anything he/she forgot to say after he/she has finished speaking

… listen for any mistakes (factual or linguistic) that A makes

… time how long it takes A to see if B can then do it more quickly.

This works well after a picture story like the one on PHOTOCOPIABLE PAGE 4.

4 Test your partner

This is the most obvious way to get students speaking together and using each other as a language practice resource.

- Students look at a page from the coursebook, and ask each other, e.g.

  A: *What's this in English?*
  B: *A house. What are these in English?*
  A: *Curtains.*

- Students walk round the classroom and ask each other about the objects there (or FLASHCARDS/posters which you've stuck on the classroom walls), e.g.

  A: *What's this in English?*
  B: *A board. What are these in English?*
  A: *Desks.*

- Students test each other on a group of known words from their vocabulary notebooks or the list at the back of the coursebook, e.g. in the lesson before an exam.

  A: *How do you say 'salchicha' in English?*
  B: *Sausage.*
  A: *Yes. How do you spell it?*
  B: *S-A-U-S-A-G-E.*

- They test each other on e.g. five words, then swap roles. You can make this competitive by getting them to score a point for each correct answer. They can do it the other way round too, e.g.

    A: *What does 'I like sausages' mean?*
    B: (answers in L1)

You can also use the mood chart on PHOTOCOPIABLE PAGE 6. Pairs or small groups have a copy of the chart in front of them.

- Student A says a phrase in one of the moods, e.g. *I want to go home.* (angrily). B just has to listen and point to the right picture (angry). Then they swap roles.

- Alternatively, A asks *How do you say 'Comment ça va?' in English?* and points to a face on the chart. The other student(s) looks at the mood, thinks of the translation and then says *How are you?* happily, quickly, etc. depending which picture was chosen. Students do this four times then swap roles.

Note: The above are all good revision activities which work best with a closed list of words, e.g. a picture dictionary page or a set of phrases.

5 Rehearse together before any 'performance'

Pairs are a safe vehicle for students to practise speaking before they do anything in front of the whole class. It allows them more time to iron out any key mistakes or problems, gives them the confidence to see that they can really do it, and makes them a little less self-conscious. Two or three Student As and two or three Bs can first prepare and rehearse together what they want to say, testing each other, clarifying doubts, etc. Then they form two or three pairs of one A and one B and do the activity as usual.

To summarise, as well as the additional speaking practice, the activities in 1 to 5 above bring further advantages.

1 Their use heightens students' expectations that they will speak English in class.
2 They really improve classroom atmosphere and help to reduce student inhibitions.
3 If you explain and teach these techniques to students, they can use them, e.g. while you're counselling or orally testing students, or outside class for homework.
4 The techniques involve no real extra work or planning for you.

Note: It's important that you use pair and groupwork for other activities too, not just speaking, so it's not alien to the students. This also helps them not to get overexcited, lose control and start babbling in L1. Students have to get used to working together, not depending on you throughout the lesson before they can start speaking together. They can do activities such as group writing or group listening, exercises, PROJECTS, etc. together rather than alone.

◆ FOR FURTHER EVERYDAY ACTIVITIES, SEE CHAPTERS 8 AND 10 TO 13

1 Tick the techniques above that you **don't** use regularly in class. Could you use any of these?
2 Which of the techniques in this chapter could your students do at home? Which do your weaker students know they could do at home?

CHAPTER 10

Controlled practice accuracy activities

A good range of speaking activities is essential for any teacher, not only because variety increases interest and motivation. Individual students will always get more from certain types of exercises than others. Students need a lot of practice if they're to learn to speak from part-time language classes and we need variety too: a bored teacher is probably not much fun to learn with!

Chapters 10 to 12 all focus on different activity types. Those in this chapter all focus on ACCURACY, i.e. students work with limited, controlled language, either in pairs or groups. They assume the particular language items in focus have already been presented and so are a follow-up stage to the drills in Chapters 6 and 7.

1 Drilling vocabulary

Some teachers tend to drill all new words more than is necessary, especially those that are easier to say. For example, when introducing colours, students don't need to repeat *red*, *black* or *green* as often as *orange*, *yellow* or *purple*. After students have heard and repeated the easier words in a group once and have been drilled in the pronunciation of any trickier ones, there are a number of interesting ways to 'drill themselves' without you having to keep modelling the words for them.

Personalising new sets of words

A good way to get students using and saying a new set of words quickly is to find ways for students to RANK them from first to last according to a given criterion, i.e. put them in some kind of order of preference. Here are some examples.

- Introduce the set on the board, e.g. sports, rooms, clothes, machines, verbs, etc. Use pictures, mime or sound effects if you can. Elicit those that students know and translate those they don't know but want to. Drill pronunciation only as necessary and mark the stress on multi-syllable words to encourage them to say them correctly, e.g. if you were teaching 'the house', on the board you might have:

study hall bedroom bathroom
kitchen toilet garage
garden living room balcony

Ask students to make a personal choice from the words on the board. They can do this either alone then tell a partner, or in conjunction with a partner to produce an agreed/combined list, e.g. you might ask the students to list the rooms in their house/flat from biggest to smallest. To do so, they have to:

… understand, process and say all the words at least once to do the activity and then again to feedback to either class or partner

… say some of them several times if their rooms are nearly the same size

… produce *I haven't got a …* if necessary.

Thus they're 'drilling themselves': repeating the words to themselves (or to a partner) with no effort on your part. This is just as effective as repetition drilling, more memorable, much more interesting and has a tangible product.

Other examples of groups to RANK include:

... their favourite three types of film, book, etc. and/or the one they like the least
... the three most expensive/cheapest/most useful machines, etc.
... the most dangerous/fun/expensive/popular sports, etc.
... the best colours for various items of clothing, etc.
... the three/five items they would save first if there was a fire, e.g. from their bedroom or living room
... the two possessions they would take with them to a desert island, etc.

You can usually find a way to get students repeating sets of words several times in order to rank them somehow. Some they'll obviously say only once to discard them, but at least they have to think about and **vocalise** each one while doing the activity, and again when they feed back. Even if much of what they say together is in L1, insist that they at least use English for the new words from the board.

Linking with words in L1

RANKING can also usefully extend to contrasting English words with words from their L1. Give students any set of new words as above, or any page of known words from their vocabulary books. Either as a whole class or first in groups and then feeding back as a class, students decide together:

... the word which sounds or looks most similar to its L1 equivalent
... the word which sounds or looks closest to an L1 word with a different meaning
... the word with the easiest/most difficult spelling
... the easiest/hardest to say/remember, etc.

T A S K

What's the next new vocabulary group you're going to teach one of your classes? Can you think of an appropriate RANKING exercise for it?

2 Noughts and crosses

● Draw on the board a *Noughts and crosses* grid with nine categories like this:

Does ... ?	Were ... ?	Are ... ?
Is ... ?	Has ... ?	Was ... ?
Did ... ?	Would ... ?	Could ... ?

● Divide the class into two equal teams. Team A plays with an 0 and Team B with an X.

● Team A chooses a square (e.g. *Could?*) and makes a sentence using the word, e.g. *Could you open the window, please?* If their sentence is correct, rub out *Could ...?* and write 0 in that square; if it's wrong, Team B has only one guess to correct it. If this is right, they win the square and you write an X in it.

● Then it's Team B's turn, etc. The first team to get a straight line of three Xs or three 0s in any direction wins the game.

You can practise many language points with *Noughts and crosses* including:

... *wh-?* questions (*What kind of ...?*, *How often ...?*, etc.)
... past tense irregular verbs, e.g. *see/go/take/get*, etc. Students have to change the verbs into the past tense and make a correct sentence
... adverbs, e.g. *yet, already, just, ago, usually, tomorrow, since, for, never*, etc.

3 Guessing games

Guessing games are a simple way to drill or revise question forms for **any** tense or vocabulary, e.g. the past tense.

- Tell students *I went somewhere yesterday.* Write where you went on a big piece of paper (e.g. McDonald's) but keep it hidden from the class.

- Ask *Can you guess where I went? You have only ten guesses.* Students have to ask questions like *Did you go (to the country/beach/a nightclub/disco?,* etc.). Insist they use the correct forms and give full answers yourself, e.g. *No, I didn't.*

- Count their guesses and build tension: *You've only got three guesses left!* If they can't guess it in ten, either tell them the answer, or give them some clues, e.g. *It begins with 'M'* or mime eating a hamburger. Dramatically reveal the name on your paper and show it to the class when they guess it.

- Students then do the same in pairs or small groups.

You can introduce an element of guessing to practise any tense as above or asking about any set of nouns. Here are some examples.

Activities: *Do you like cycling/skating/playing computer games?* etc.
Small objects: *Have you got a hankie/key/rubber? ... any keys/money?*, etc.

4 Splash

This involves word prompts on the board to drill tenses, e.g. *Do you ...? Did you ...? Are you going to ...?* Ask the class to tell you things they can or can't do and put them on the board. But don't write them as a list. Instead, 'splash' them on the board at angles so there's no logical order to read them in. Otherwise, students will automatically start at the top of the list and read down as we're trained to do all our lives. For example:

In pairs, students ask and answer any or all of these questions, depending on their level and your focus: *How often do you (wash your hair)? Did you (wash your hair) yesterday? Are you going to (wash your hair) tomorrow? Do you like (washing your hair)?*

Because there's no obvious order, they can't predict which question is coming next and so have to listen to their partner. You can always supply the phrases to practise yourself, but students get much more involved if you ask them. And it's easy to slip in a few specific ones that you want to revise!

You can obviously use a list of prompts like this on paper too. If you do, the Splash layout is much better than a vertical list.

5 Spidergrams

Again, these can be prompts on the board or on paper. Students are given a series of word or picture prompts around a theme, to provide a skeleton for a question/answer exchange, as in the example on the next page.

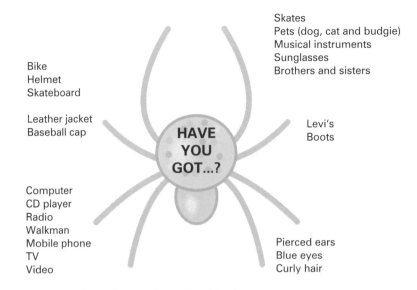

Skates
Pets (dog, cat and budgie)
Musical instruments
Sunglasses
Brothers and sisters

Bike
Helmet
Skateboard

Leather jacket
Baseball cap

HAVE YOU GOT...?

Levi's
Boots

Computer
CD player
Radio
Walkman
Mobile phone
TV
Video

Pierced ears
Blue eyes
Curly hair

Make sure students know they should ask:

Have you got a ...? with the words on the left
Have you got any ...? with those on the right
Have you got ...? with the last three.

They can ask in circular order around the SPIDERGRAM, or in random order.

There is a pictorial version of this on PHOTOCOPIABLE PAGE 7. On the same page is a second SPIDERGRAM to practise past tense questions and talking about holidays.

6 Revolving circles

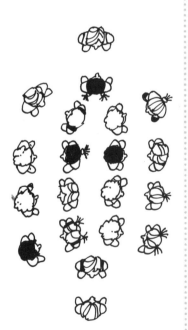

For this activity, you need to clear a large space in the classroom, or play it in the gym, hall or outside in the playground.

- Provide some word prompts, either on the board or on a piece of paper. This is a good revision activity at the beginning of the academic year, when you might put general prompts like these on the board:

name   brothers/sisters   flat   hobbies
parents   favourite sports/music/TV programmes
phone number   grandparents   live

- Elicit some questions for each topic, e.g. *Where do you live? How many brothers and sisters have you got? What does your father do/look like?*, etc.

- Divide the class in half. Each half forms two circles, one inside the other. The outer circle faces inwards, the inner circle faces outwards so they're looking at each other, as in the example on the left.

- Those in the inner circle face those in the outer circle to form pairs. They ask and answer as many questions as they can for a minute. Then clap your hands and the outer circle revolves clockwise, so students change partners. This way students meet and talk to half the class in a fun, lively way, while you're free to monitor and help (or join the circle yourself if you've got uneven numbers).

- Combine this activity with a SPIDERGRAM whenever you want a longer, more intensive speaking drill. It's particularly good for getting students to mix with and talk to a new partner. Here's another example. Write on the board:

What have we got in common?
brothers   sisters   pairs of sunglasses   pets   grandparents
radios   phones   computers   beds   TVs   rooms in your flat

- Students have a minute with each partner in the circle to find out who they've got most in common with, asking *How many (sisters) have you got?*, etc.

7 Mingling

For any question/answer exchange, students can practise first in groups with the students near them, and then stand up, move around and ask the whole class. This is called MINGLING. MINGLE drills are one of the best ways to practise any structure orally, present, past or future, or personal information questions, whether factual or to do with tastes. They can link with any class survey type activity (SEE 8 BELOW). There are several ways to do them.

Asking the same questions

Students can all ask the same questions to complete a personal copy of the information, e.g. a class phone book.

Name	Phone number
Marina	3414903
Macarena	3579508
Toni	3347758

Students ask each other *What's your name?* and *What's your phone number?* They list everybody's name and phone number to build a group or class 'phone book'.

Asking different questions

Students ask different questions from prompts to as many others in the class as possible in a given time limit. Here are two examples.

Skeleton prompts

Each student has SKELETON PROMPTS to complete with an item of their choice, either copied from the board or on slips of paper, e.g.

> *Do you like _____? (the name of a famous pop star)*
>
> *Do you often eat _____? (the name of your favourite sweets)*
>
> *Do you like shopping at _____? (a shop you think is terrible)*

Students choose a name to complete the question, according to the prompts, then mingle and ask other students, and answer their questions too.

It's easy to apply this to other structures too. Students can always add one or two questions of their own, if you're prepared to help them to translate their ideas, e.g. for the present perfect:

> *Have you ever been to a football match at _____? (the name of a bad football stadium)*
>
> *Have you ever seen _____? (the name of a bad film)*
> *Have you ever _____? (you invent the question)*

Sentence stems

Dictate some unfinished sentences (or 'stems') for students to complete, e.g. to practise seasons, months and dates.

My birthday is in ...	*My mother's birthday is ...*
My birthday is on ...	*My favourite season is ...*

Students write them down and then complete the sentences with true answers. Then they mingle to find the student in the class who has the most similar answers to them for each question.

Assuming responsibility for one question

Students (or pairs/small groups) can each be responsible for one question to ask the rest of the class. Here is an example for a class of 33 students.

- Divide the class into eleven groups of three students (A, B and C). Give each group a different question, e.g. from *Are you a TV addict?* (SEE PHOTOCOPIABLE PAGE 12) or from the class survey started below.

- Re-divide them into three groups of eleven Student As, eleven Student Bs and eleven Student Cs. Each student has to ask all the other students in their new group their question, and note the results.

- When they've finished, the original groups come back together, combine their results and thus produce a survey of the entire class.

8 Class surveys

Class surveys work well if you add a guessing element. According to the language you want to practise, produce a grid like this:

How many people in this class ...?	My guess	Real number
... are left-handed? ... have got a crash helmet? ... like spicy food? ... have been abroad?		

- Draw it on the board for students to copy. Tell them the total number of students in the class, including you if you want to join in.

- Ask them to guess how many of the class are left-handed. They have to write their guess in the first column, e.g. 10. Repeat for the other questions.

- Subdivide the class into groups, e.g. four groups: W, X, Y and Z, e.g. according to their rows of seats. Students stand up and ask everybody in their group *Are you left-handed? Have you got a crash helmet?*, etc. and note down the answers. All they do is repeat the same questions so even the weaker students should manage and the competitive element adds a layer of fun.

- Once they've asked everybody, get individual students to tell you the total number from their group for each question, e.g. Group W = 2, Group X = 3, etc.

- Add up the totals with the students, who write down each of the real number totals in the second column. At the end ask *How many did you guess correctly?* to see who 'won'. ◆ FOR MORE GAMES SEE CHAPTERS 11 AND 12

Try to devise one or more of the following:

... a guessing game to practise the next lexical set you have to teach

... a MINGLE drill to practise the next structure you have to teach

... a SPIDERGRAM or a class survey to revise the different tenses one of your classes knows.

Give a copy to a colleague to try out, and ask for feedback.

CHAPTER 11

Information-gap activities

"Which are the best speaking activities?"

The best are those that:

1 are **relevant** to students' interests, stimulate them to want to talk and are at the right language level.

2 contain an **element of choice** as to how students can do them and what they say, to allow them to express their own personalities at least a little.

3 are **localised** and often made or adapted by the teacher who knows his/her students best. It's always a good idea to personalise and customise coursebook exercises where possible, using pictures, local names, faces and places to replace those in the book. Here are two examples.

- Rather than just doing what's in the coursebook, e.g. to introduce giving opinions, do a heads-up FLASHCARD presentation, such as:

  What do you think of ...? (FLASHCARD of a local place)
  What do you think of ...? (FLASHCARD of a locally famous person)
  What do you think of ...? (FLASHCARD of a sportsperson students know)

- Alternatively, for comparatives, two FLASHCARDS of a pop star and a sports hero, for example, for students to compare who's taller, fatter, thinner, stronger, more intelligent, etc. ◆ SEE CHAPTER 5 FOR MORE PRESENTATION IDEAS

4 force students to listen to each other. ◆ SEE PAGE 47

5 have a clear objective, e.g. a problem needing to be solved, so they know when they've finished and achieved what you asked.

6 contain an INFORMATION or OPINION GAP.

"What's an information gap?"

Each student has or is given information that his/her partner doesn't have. Students have to interact in order to share their information, in other words to 'bridge the gap' between them. Good speaking exercises have either an INFORMATION GAP (I can't complete the exercise until I get the information which my partner has) or an OPINION GAP (I don't know what you think so I have to ask and listen to find out), e.g. two students have to plan a route somewhere but one student can see only a train timetable and the other a bus timetable. Each has to tell the other the information they have in order for them to decide how best to travel.

Language practice is much more meaningful when students are asking questions to which they don't already know the answers. Compare with the traditional alternative, where students were drilled or drilled themselves from information they both already knew or could see. If both students have the same timetable, there's little point in A asking B *What time does the train leave?* when A can see for him/herself!

TASK

Think about your favourite speaking activity. Does it satisfy criteria 1 to 6 above?

1 Creating an information gap

There are some very good published INFORMATION-GAP activities. ◈ SEE FURTHER READING Here are some very simple ways for you to generate such activities.

Information gap on the board

Put words or pictures on the board, or BLU-TACK things on it, e.g. posters, FLASHCARDS, etc. One student looks at the information on the board, the other(s) simply looks away or sits with their backs to the board. ◈ SEE THE DESCRIBING GAME PAGE 66

Information gap from books/the teacher

In pairs or groups, one student has the information from:

… a whispered word or slip of paper from the teacher

… the coursebook (all students have their books closed, except one student who can see a picture, list of words, etc.)

… the coursebook interaction section (most modern coursebooks have A/B communication activities, which supply different information for students in pairs to complete together).

Information gap from real materials

● Look for a suitable text from a newspaper, magazine, brochure, etc. containing 'real' facts, e.g. cinema information, advertisements, articles, biographies.

● Make two copies and, using correction fluid, blank different words out in each one. Mark one copy A and the other B.

● Make copies for each pair (A and B). Students ask each other questions, e.g. *What time does the film start/finish? What's on at the New Theatre? When was Madonna born?*, etc. to complete their information.

This can also be done with dialogues, e.g.

A	B
I went to the ..... with John.	*I went to the ice-rink with .....*
A asks *Where did she go?*	B asks *Who did she go with?*

Note: If your students are weak at formulating questions, As can work together in pairs beforehand to prepare the questions, as can Bs.

Cover the text below and look back through the activities in Chapter 10. How many of them contain an INFORMATION GAP? Label those that do. Then check your answer below.

Unless students already know the answers to the questions they're asking (e.g. *What's your name?* to somebody they know or *Do you like football?* to a known avid fan), the answer is that they all do.

2 Home-made information-gap activities

As with presentation techniques (SEE PAGE 28), pictures are invaluable. Here are three ways to exploit a simple, home-made picture.

Find the same picture

- Draw a simple scene ten times. ◈ SEE PHOTOCOPIABLE PAGE 8 Each picture has one small difference from all the others. This could be:
    … a different item or number of items
    … an item in a different position
    … a different shade (black or white) or pattern.
- Photocopy the sheet once for every ten students in your class, e.g. with a class of 40, make four copies, cut them up and give each student a picture, which they mustn't show to anybody else.
- Pre-teach any new words, putting them on the board if necessary. The advantage of drawing your own is choosing which words are practised.
- Students describe their picture to other students in the class and ask questions until they find another student who has exactly the same picture. They use language like *On the right there's a black cat. Have you got a black cat? How many birds are there? Is your door white?*, etc.

Spot the difference

Perhaps the best speaking activity of all, this is a reliable friend that works at any level. At my school in Spain, I regularly had to substitute for sick teachers without notice. I always kept a supply of three different spot-the-difference pictures to hand so I could just walk in and, according to the level, do the easy one, the intermediate one or the difficult one. This guaranteed me a good first 20 minutes and enough time to invent something else for the rest of the lesson!

- Give each student a picture from PHOTOCOPIABLE PAGE 8. They turn to the person next to them to find the number of differences between their pictures, using similar language to *Find the same picture* above. Then they can turn to another partner and do it again.

Many ready-made commerical versions of this are available and you can sometimes find examples in your local press and puzzle books too. The disadvantage of not drawing your own is that you have less control over the vocabulary. As this is such a good activity, there are two more spot the differences on PHOTOCOPIABLE PAGE 9.

Describe and draw

One student looks at a picture and describes it to his/her partner, who has to draw it, without seeing it. You can do this with PHOTOCOPIABLE PAGE 8 again. This involves language like *Draw a black cat in the right-hand corner at the bottom. There are three birds flying outside the window*, etc. Once the drawing is complete the students compare it with the original, which is usually fun. Then they swap roles.

Pictionary

Use the commercial game Pictionary to practise speaking in the class, or play a simplified version practising vocabulary and phrases of your choice.

- Choose about ten vocabulary items/phrases you want to practise, e.g. names of animals, present continuous phrases such as *He's swimming*. Write the items onto cards several times.

- Put the class into teams of about five students. Give each team a set of cards.
- In turn, members of each team pick the first card and have to draw what's on it. The other team members mustn't see it. They have to guess what their partner is drawing and say the exact words on the card, i.e. **not** *He swims*.
- When they guess the word(s) on the card, the next team member takes the next card and draws it, etc. The team to guess all the words first wins the game.

Find someone who ...

This is one of the most common and popular activities in English Language Teaching today. You can use this to practise a specific tense or to revise mixed structures, e.g. just before an exam. Although many published ones are available, the best are those that:

- you make yourself, containing exactly the language you wish to practise, including the names of locally famous, controversial/fun people and places.
- include a second column to make students ask FOLLOW-UP QUESTIONS, to progress beyond interrogation into more natural conversation and FLUENCY.

Look at PHOTOCOPIABLE PAGE 10. Help students to fill the chart in with questions they want to ask the class, as in the sample below. Give and elicit suggestions for each line, then help them to translate and fill in their ideas.

Find someone who ...

	name	details
can swim 100 metres	Marco	He says it's easy!
can't make an omelette	Julia	She can't cook.
likes Johnny Depp	Oscar	good actor
doesn't like studying English	Alba	difficult
has got a tattoo	Pepa	on her arm
hasn't got a Disney video	....	....
would like to have a lot of children when they leave school	....	....
went to the cinema last weekend	....	....
didn't do the last homework	....	....
has been to the beach recently	....	....
hasn't been to McDonald's	....	....
is going to earn some money soon	....	....
isn't going to do anything this weekend	....	....
is the tallest person in their family	....	....
is going to cycle home	....	....
played basketball last week	....	....

(The idea of adding FOLLOW-UP QUESTIONS came from Christina Latham-Koenig.)

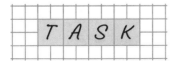

TASK

Which activities in Chapter 10 are not suitable for home-made adaption and production similar to those above? (SEE PAGE 96 FOR THE ANSWER)

CHAPTER 12

Freer and fluency practice activities

There are many good free-speaking games and activities. ◆ SEE FURTHER READING Below are the best ones I've found for lower levels. They're ordered from more to less controlled, the latter few all practising pure FLUENCY.

Note: Remember you have to explain and demonstrate them yourself clearly first before asking students to play them together. ◆ SEE PAGE 46

1 Read, predict, uncover and check

This is an easy way to get students speaking from a reading text and much more fun than reading aloud. Use PHOTOCOPIABLE PAGE 11.

● Make and give out a copy per pair (or one each if your school can afford it!). Tell students to cover the text and look only at the pictures. Ask *What can you see in the pictures? What do you know about James Bond?* and elicit answers. Use the opportunity to elicit/pre-teach the necessary English words.

● Demonstrate that they should uncover the text line by line as you read it aloud. They must not read beyond each question. Read the first paragraph until you reach question 1, then elicit their answers. You'll know at once if they've cheated as they'll just call out the first line of the next paragraph. Elicit all the answers you can, then ask students to read the answer.

● Repeat this procedure for each paragraph, with students uncovering the story as you read it. They should stop and guess each time you reach a question, until you get to the end. The answer to the last question is *fell in love with James Bond*.

● You can easily adapt this technique for any story. Simply retype the story, inserting questions at appropriate points in the same way.

2 Glug

This is a good game to revise verbs and tenses, especially short answers.

● Play *Glug* in groups of three or four. The first student chooses a verb or verb phrase, e.g. *have a shower*.

● The others have to guess what it is by making sentences which use the invented verb *glug* to replace the chosen mystery verb.

A: *OK, I'm ready.*
B: *Are you glugging now?*
A: *No, I'm not.*
C: *Do you glug every day?*
A: *Yes, I do.*
D: *Did you glug this morning?*
A: *Yes, I did.*
C: *Can you glug in the kitchen?*
A: *No, I can't.*
B: *Can you glug in the bathroom?*
A: *Yes, I can.*
D: *Is it 'clean your teeth'?*
A: *No, it isn't.*
B: *Is it 'have a shower'?*
A: *Yes!*

● The student who guesses the verb then has a turn.

3 Twenty questions

This is a more advanced guessing game than the ones in Chapter 10. Students have to guess the identity of a mystery person, practising question formation, nationalities, jobs and adjectives.

- Play the game in groups or as a class. Write the names of famous people on cards. One student draws a card and assumes that person's identity. The others have up to 20 questions to find out who it is.
- The student with the card can only answer *Yes, (I am.)/No, (I'm not.)* or *I don't know.* If they don't know, the question doesn't count.
- Elicit and splash on the board the kind of questions students have to ask, e.g.

> Are you alive/dead? Are you a man/woman? Are you an actor/a singer? Are you married/divorced? Are you (Spanish/from Madrid)? Have you got any children? Are you (Claudia Schiffer)? Is your boyfriend (Julio Iglesias)?

- The student who guesses correctly draws the next famous name, and so on.

This is also good for guessing a job, e.g. *Do you work indoors/with your hands? Do you have to drive/wear a uniform?* Again, practise some of the questions first.

4 A video letter

If you're lucky enough to have a camcorder in the school, students can make a 'video letter' to another class or students at a neighbouring school. (This can also obviously be done with audio cassettes.)

- Give (or let them choose) a topic, e.g. Our town, Our class, Our hobbies, etc.
- Help them to prepare what they want to say, then record them doing so.
- Pass the video onto the appropriate class and wait for a reply. If both classes enjoy it, this can develop into regular 'video correspondence'.

(I was introduced to this activity by Kenny Graham.)

5 The describing game

One of the best FLUENCY games, this practises the vital language skills of defining and paraphrase when you don't know a word in English, e.g.

It's a place where ...   *It's an adjective.*   *It's a thing you use to ...*
You find it in the ...   *It's an animal ...*   *It's a person who ...*

You can use it to practise any vocabulary group or for general vocabulary revision.

- Put students into pairs, A and B. Students A turn round so that they can't see the board. The Bs can see the board.
- Write seven words on the board, e.g.

  banana   Madonna   sugar   blue   twelve   a pilot   passport

- B has to describe the first word to A without using the word, and speaking only in English, e.g. *It's a fruit. It's long and yellow. It comes from Africa./ She's a singer. She's American. She's very rich and famous.*
- A listens and guesses the word he/she thinks it is. If the guess is correct, B then defines the second word. If it's wrong, B has to try to give a clearer definition.
- If they find it hard at first, teach them to give the first letter as a clue, e.g. *It begins with B.*
- When all the pairs have finished, students swap roles. Write seven new words on the board and continue.

6 Crazy stories

Make up a reading or listening text full of mistakes, like the one below. (Listening is better for this activity.)

How many stupid mistakes did I make yesterday?

Yesterday morning I got up at eight-thirty. I got dressed, and then I had a shower. At seven-thirty I went to the bus stop, and got the train to work. I worked until one o'clock, and then I had breakfast in a restaurant. I finished work at five o'clock, and then I went shopping in the park. At six-thirty I met my boyfriend, and we went to the theatre to see a film. Afterwards, we had a drink in the post office, then we walked home in my car and we got home at midday.

- Ask *How many stupid mistakes did I make yesterday? Listen.* Then read it aloud quite slowly for the class to get the general idea.
- Repeat your question and read it again for them to count your mistakes.
- Put them in pairs to compare and count the mistakes they spotted.
- Ask *How many?* and see which pair spotted the highest number of mistakes. (There are nine.) Ask them to try to say all that they can in English.
- Read the text one more time, line by line, and elicit the mistakes each time.

Here's another example. This time tell students the name of the story they're going to hear (Cinderella). Tell the class to listen and find twelve mistakes in the story (in bold below). Read the story twice, students compare in pairs and then feed back, as above.

Once upon a time there was a girl called Cinderella who lived with her two **brothers**. *They were very* **beautiful**. *Cinderella worked in the house, and her sisters* **helped her**. *One day, an invitation arrived to a* **disco** *at the king's palace. Cinderella's sisters went to the party, and they said 'You* **can** *come to the party, Cinderella.' Suddenly, Cinderella's fairy* **godfather** *appeared. 'You can go to the party, Cinderella,' she said, and she gave her a* **leather jacket** *and a* **motorbike**. *At the party, Cinderella danced with the* **king**, *but at* **half past eleven** *she had to leave and run home. When she ran, she left her* **handbag**. *The prince looked for Cinderella and, finally, he found her, and* **they went to the USA** *together.*

This can obviously be adapted for any locally well-known story or legend.

7 Listen and raise your hand if it's true for you

This is my favourite listening activity. Students listen to sentences from you and:

… raise their left hand if it's true for them
… raise their right hand if it's false for them
… cross their hands if they're not sure.

For example, if you say *I'm a boy*, all the boys in the class should raise their left hand because it's true for them, and the girls their right hands. Anyone with their hands crossed has got a problem!

You can focus on any language area:

… adjectives: *I'm tired, hot, hungry*, etc.
… nouns, e.g. clothes: *I'm wearing shoes, trainers, boots, sandals*, etc.
… tenses: *I went out last night, I saw a film, I had a pizza*, etc.

This activity works well because it has a physical response, which uses up some energy; students don't have to say anything so it's nice and quiet (in theory!) and you can see who understands and who needs help.

Once you've done this a few times, and demonstrated clearly, students can do the same thing together as a speaking and listening activity.

- Put them in small groups of four or five. Elect one student to begin, e.g. *I'm wearing something black. I'm wearing something blue*, etc.

- The rest of the group listens and raises or crosses their hands accordingly.

- After a few sentences it's the turn of the next student to choose some sentences. Again, they can revise a particular language point, e.g. *going to*: *I'm going to watch TV tonight, I'm not going to do my homework*, or it can be general revision.

8 Talking about topics

It's easy to pick topics and invent simple questionnaires as the basis for speaking activities, e.g. PHOTOCOPIABLE PAGE 12 *Are you a TV addict?* This is a pair or groupwork questionnaire to prompt conversation about TV, video and radio.

- Copy one questionnaire per pair or per student.

- Focus on the pictures. Ask *What can you see? What types of programme are they?*, etc.

- Go through questions 1–20 and make sure students understand them. Tell the class to ask you the questions first to check their pronunciation. Your answers will also help them to think about what they can say.

- Put students in pairs or small groups. Give Student A the sheet to ask B all the questions (B mustn't see the paper), then swap, telling B to ask them in a different order. This makes it more mechanical but is easier for students.

- Alternatively, to make it more like real conversation, A asks B the first question. B answers and says *What about you?* Then B asks A the second question, etc. Make sure they both know that they should ask FOLLOW-UP QUESTIONS if they can.

- Monitor and help as necessary. Then elicit feedback from the whole class.

Topics for which you can produce similar questionnaires include music, films, fashion, sport, food, i.e. anything your students will be interested in. Just list a range of simple questions to answer. Insist that students ask FOLLOW-UP QUESTIONS to provide good FLUENCY practice.

9 The speaking game

There are many board games to prompt FLUENCY and freer speaking. You can find one on PHOTOCOPIABLE PAGE 13. This has the following advantages.

With correction fluid you can blank out any topics you don't like (or that your students can't talk about), and replace them with easier ones.

The board design means that students go round in different directions, so they're all talking about different topics.

- Make one copy for each group of four students in your class and make sure each group has a coin to toss. (Some groups can have five players.)

- Each player needs a marker (a paper clip, or a bit of paper) which they put on the Start/Finish square. They all move out from the centre in a different direction. Tell students to start in the alphabetical order of their names or surnames, or according to their ages, from youngest to oldest.

- The first student tosses a coin.
  Heads = move two squares.   Tails = move one square.

- He/she has to talk for at least 30 seconds about the topic on the square, e.g. for the topic pets, *I haven't got any pets but my uncle's got a dog. His name's Wolf. He's brown. I like him. I want a dog. But I don't like cats.*

- Other students listen, time the speaker with a watch, and help, e.g. by asking questions or noticing mistakes, which they tell the student after he/she's finished. However, emphasise that mistakes aren't important. The aim is to keep talking, saying as much as they can about each topic in English.

- The game stops when the nominal 'winner' completes half a circuit around the board and returns to the middle again.

- Monitor and note the types of mistakes students are making, but don't interrupt or you'll inhibit FLUENCY. Tell students not to stop at 30 seconds if they're saying something interesting. If students like the game, play it again, raising the time limit to 45 or even 60 seconds.

10 Extra cards for roleplays

Most teachers use ROLEPLAYS to follow up situational dialogues, e.g. At the shops; students play the shop assistant and the customer and buy different items from those in the original coursebook model. Many teachers naturally add a bit of context and mime activity to these to add reality and fun, e.g. pretend to give objects and money to each other when they're shopping.

These usually work well the first time if you just let students copy the original dialogue. But when it comes to swapping roles and doing it a second time, it can get repetitive. Here are some ideas.

If you use rolecards, it will force students to improvise and practise FLUENCY.

- Students ROLEPLAY the waiter and the customer in a restaurant, following the original dialogue. They then swap roles. You give the waiter an extra card, e.g.

> *You're tired and want to go home as quickly as possible.*

> *You're poor and need a good tip. Be the perfect waiter.*

> *There's no more fish. There's only one piece of chicken left and it's very small.*

> *You want people to order the strawberries, because there are a lot left in the kitchen.*

- Alternatively, if students are ROLEPLAYING shopping for food, give the customer an extra card:

> *You haven't got any money with you.*

> *You think the shop assistant is giving you bad vegetables.*

Or the shop assistant:

> *You're in a hurry. You want to close the shop because you want to go to your brother's wedding.*

> *You haven't got any bags.*

- If they're ROLEPLAYING taking something back to the shop, give the shop assistant an extra form to fill in before they can give a refund:

HAROLD'S OF KENSINGTON

Customer's name: _____

Address: _____

Item: _____

Price: _____

Paid: cash ☐ cheque ☐ credit card ☐

Date of purchase: _____

Problem: _____

Customer's signature: _____

It's easy to add an extra ingredient for students to be communicating in a less predictable, more enjoyable way. As you can see above, many of the ideas involve adding a small problem. Ideas like these will often occur to you as you're teaching, and it's easy to write down something quickly on a slip of paper and give it to students. To find out which ones work best you have to experiment, but you can usually think of typical problems either from your own real-life experience of the situation or from TV, films, etc.

11 Can you cope ...? activities

These are often called 'deep-end activities', taking their name from what happens when you're pushed into a swimming pool: you either sink or swim. Students can often cope in a situation which they have rehearsed in class, but naturally have more problems when faced with an unexpected situation, as in real life. Give the students real-life situations for them to practise in class, e.g.

A *You're a tourist in England. You don't like English food. You're very, very hungry. Ask somebody in the street for help.*

B *You're English. You're walking down the street when a tourist stops you. You only speak English.*

A *You've left your school bag on the bus. It's full of things. Go to the police station. Tell the police officer.*

B *You're an English police officer. You only speak English. Take all A's details.*

◆ SEE PHOTOCOPIABLE PAGE 14 FOR MORE EXAMPLES

A good way to try them is to keep a set copied and cut up in your register and use them occasionally for five or ten-minute 'fillers'. Choose only those that you think your students can cope with.

These provide opportunities for real communication and FLUENCY practice, similar to the sunglasses idea (SEE PAGE 18). The subjects chosen needn't be related to the content of the coursebook unit they're studying at the time.

- Pre-teach only the words on the cards.

- Put students in groups/pairs of only As and only Bs to prepare a few ideas together and perhaps encourage some note-taking.

- Impress upon students that this is a FLUENCY activity. Their success is not measured by the number of correct English sentences produced but by their ability to cope and communicate, using all the means at their disposal: their hands, noises, mime, drawing, anything, as if they were lost in the middle of a country where only English is spoken.

- When students have finished, ask them to give themselves scores from 0–3 as below. Translate and put this scoring system on the board.

> 0 = No communication at all. We couldn't do anything.
> 1 = We communicated a little of what we wanted to say, but not much.
> 2 = We communicated fairly well, but couldn't say a lot in English.
> 3 = We understood each other, spoke some English and did it quite well.

- Then they can ask you to teach them any words they needed to say, and perhaps swap roles and do it again with another partner, so it's less predictable.

TASK

At the start of this chapter, we said that the activities were RANKED in terms of the level of FLUENCY required (SEE PAGE 65). Do you agree with this order?

CHAPTER 13

Oral homework

Traditionally, students have practised listening and speaking only in class. Homework has usually involved reading and writing. Most workbooks contain only written tasks, mainly because they're straightforward to write and easy to mark.

Students will not take speaking seriously if it's only an occasional classroom activity and never part of their homework or evaluation. ◆ SEE CHAPTER 14 Besides, two or three class hours a week doesn't allow enough time for students to learn to speak with any confidence. If our aim is to help students to speak, then the type of homework we set should reflect this.

Given how little class time is available and how much more students can achieve for themselves outside class given the right tasks, it's well worth investing class time in preparing, organising, monitoring and correcting homework. With a little imagination, we can easily devise simple oral homework activities.

Cover the list below. Can you think of any ways to get your students speaking outside class?

Here are some ideas.

1 Use a workbook with oral exercises and a self-study cassette

If a workbook has no pronunciation or speaking tasks, it isn't really appropriate for a course whose aim is to teach spoken English. Perhaps you could choose another one, or at least try to supplement the activities in the workbook.

Many courses now have workbook cassettes, but teachers often don't use these because of the extra cost. If at all possible, it **is** worth using them as they involve no extra work for us and offer a wonderful opportunity for weaker students in particular to get extra practice. If students get no speaking practice outside the class, the message they receive is that speaking isn't so important.

Note: if a particular course that you like doesn't have a cassette, ask the publisher to produce one! If enough teachers ask, they usually will.

2 Homework partners

Traditionally, students doing homework together has been seen as 'cheating'. While this may be considered the case with some subjects, e.g. maths, or an exam exercise, it need not be the case with language learning. On the contrary, it's one way of guaranteeing students speak outside class.

Students do homework in pairs

Tell students to choose a homework partner, i.e. one of their friends. They should try to do homework together, e.g. workbook exercises, revision, even practising dialogues. At least they can compare answers before it is checked. The advantage of this is that students inevitably have to vocalise some words when they do so; even if they're only doing a gap-fill exercise, one student has to say the missing word to his/her partner, thus encouraging them to think about how words are said.

Homework partners could also be made responsible for passing on lesson notes, photocopies/handouts, homework information, etc. in the case of absence, so nobody has an excuse for missing anything (in theory at least!). This should encourage students to be more responsible and autonomous too.

Students do projects in groups

This applies equally to PROJECT-type homework. Here, students in groups research and write up their PROJECT together, using reference materials such as dictionaries, encyclopaedias, interviews with local people, etc. Any group-type activity where they have to share results will ensure at least a minimum of verbalisation as students have to compare results and agree what to write together. Here are some ideas.

- Ask students to plan a perfect day out for the class, then write it up for everyone to choose the best idea.
- Students find out about the energy/protein/carbohydrate content of certain kinds of food, then report to others.
- They find out the oldest, highest, most expensive, etc. place in town.
- They write up articles for a class magazine, etc.

3 Teach techniques that students can use outside class

Students test themselves

Encourage students to record words and phrases in such a way that they can easily cover them with another book or a separate sheet of paper and then test themselves, e.g. in two columns:

English	L1
We went to the country.	Fuimos al campo.
farmer	granjero
farm	granja
tractor	tractor

Spend time in class establishing and practising this technique. Set students a page of words to learn and test them next lesson. Demonstrate how they can also do the same with a picture dictionary, which weaker students in particular may find useful.

Students test a partner

Similarly, teach students ways that they can test another student in order to practise together. Demonstrate this in class first to make sure they know what to do, e.g.

A: How do you say (campo) in English?
B: Country.
A: What does (farmer) mean?
B: Granjero.

Then set it as a regular task. This is also a useful, in-class pairwork technique for initial practice and consolidation of a large number of new words.

Students mark and practise the stress on new words

Most students keep a word list of some kind. However, unless the list provides some help with pronunciation, it's of limited value. It teaches no more than spelling and translation and doesn't encourage students to want to say the words. That's why, for example, travel phrasebooks always have a phonetic-type transcription beside the words: they'd be of little use without them.

If you can always remember to mark the stress yourself when you introduce a new word on the board, you can then ask students to do the same. If you're halfway through the year and haven't been marking the stress, teach students how to do it, e.g. by underlining or with a box above the stressed syllable, e.g.

<u>ham</u>burger   ham☐burger

Then, ask students in groups to look back over their own word lists and mark the stress on all multi-syllable words. You'll probably be surprised by how unsure they are. From now on, try to get them to mark the stress regularly and practise saying the words with the correct stress when they test themselves at home. Teach and insist that students use these phrases in class:

Where's the stress on (farmer)?
How do you pronounce (country)?

Students can play games together in English

Many common teaching games can easily be played by students outside class, e.g. *Hangman, Bingo, Buzz, Simon says*, anagrams, guessing games. Indeed students often play games like *Spoof* in the playground anyway, so why not suggest they play in English instead of their L1? (In this game each player in a team of three has up to three coins in one closed hand, which they hold out in front of them: they have to guess the total number they're holding between them. This only involves saying the numbers from 0 to 9 plus *It's your turn. Come on. What did you say? Who said four?*)

Another example is *Word tennis*, which students can play in pairs (or groups) to revise any vocabulary group, e.g. animals. Student A serves with *cat*, B responds with *elephant*, A returns with *dog*, B with *lion*, etc. until one student can't think of a word in English from the group. Then they choose another word group, e.g. drinks, vegetables, question words, adjectives and play again.

If your students particularly enjoyed playing any of these games in class, why not set them for homework? Of course your telling them to do so will in no way guarantee that they do, but at least by suggesting it you've given them the idea and one or two students might. They certainly won't if you don't suggest it!

4 Re-processing their own word lists

Think back to the vocabulary notebooks you filled as a language student at secondary school. Apart from just before an exam, how often did you look at them? Teachers don't often come up with tasks to help students look back over their word lists apart from the general instruction to 'revise constantly', yet this is an essential step in helping students, particularly the weaker ones to catch up and remember. Here are some ideas.

Classify words by the common sound

Ask students working alone or in pairs/groups to look through their books and find three words which have the same sound, either vowels or consonants, e.g.

w**or**d	**are**	T**ue**sday
ch**ur**ch	f**a**ther	f**oo**d
b**ir**thday	h**a**lf	n**ew**

or

jam	**g**lasses	**y**ear
Germany	ba**g**	**y**oung
en**j**oy	ma**g**azine	**u**niversity

This makes students look for patterns and think about the relationship between spelling and pronunciation. Above all, it actually forces them to say the words. Elicit feedback from the students, write the words they've found onto the board and you will have the beginnings of a 'Sound dictionary'. This will help students see some of the common spelling and pronunciation patterns.

Classify words by the number of syllables and stress pattern

Ask students to look through their books and find three words which have:

1 two syllables with the stress on the first syllable
2 two syllables with the stress on the second syllable
3 three syllables with the stress on the first syllable
4 three syllables with the stress on the second syllable
5 three syllables with the stress on the third syllable, etc.

1 ■ □	2 □ ■	3 ■ □□	4 □ ■□	5 □ □ ■
football	cassette	alphabet	computer	afternoon
orange	divorced	hospital	detective	understand
evening	because	elephant	musician	margarine

This makes students look for pronunciation and spelling patterns and forces them to say the words. Combining lists on the board can produce quite a large number of words for each pattern and give you an interesting insight into students' awareness of syllables, stress and pronunciation in general. Perhaps the best thing about exercises like this is that students cannot translate when looking at pronunciation patterns: they have to think in English.

5 Memorisation

When I was twelve, I started studying Russian. Once we'd learned the alphabet, the teacher gave us an 18-line dialogue to memorise. I can still repeat it today, 27 years later! Whether it was because I liked the teacher or because it took such an effort, I don't know. Whatever the reason, the technique obviously worked.

Although 'unfashionable', memorisation is a valid, extremely useful way both for students to learn and for us to check that they've done so. Therefore, encourage students to learn a dialogue, picture story, key phrases, irregular verb tables, etc. It forces students to practise repeating words and to think about pronunciation outside class. It's also a low-threat activity and an easy way to begin speaking in class. Students don't have to think or invent language; they simply repeat other people's words. Here are some ways to check learning.

- Ask students to perform the dialogue in class either to a partner or in front of the class, alone or in pairs.
- Alternatively, you can go round and ask individual students to perform while the rest are doing a written exercise (see 6 Password below).
- Don't forget to re-use known picture stories, dialogues, etc. that students memorised earlier in the term as part of their final evaluation. They offer an easy test for you to prepare and are motivating for students.

Note: Don't overdo memorisation or students may think it's the only way you expect them to learn.

6 Password

Tell students they won't be allowed to sit down in class next lesson if they can't say the 'password', i.e. whatever you've asked them to memorise. Next lesson, as they come in, tell them to remain standing. Each student has to say the password correctly before he/she can sit down.

You can also do this before students leave the class. If a particularly tricky word (e.g. *Wednesday*) or phrase (e.g. *I'm quite tired.*) comes up, for fun at the end of a lesson, tell students that it's the 'password' and they can't leave the classroom until they've said it correctly. Stand by the door and insist they say it to you correctly before they leave. If they get it right they can go, if not, they return to the back of the queue and try again!

This is also fun with 'tongue twisters' for sounds which your students find particularly difficult, e.g. *Thursday the thirteenth is my mother's thirty-fifth birthday!*

7 Cassette-based tasks

Students can easily practise at home with a cassette recorder. They only need to:

… record themselves

… play it back and listen to how they sound.

While you may think most of your students wouldn't do this, they certainly won't if you don't suggest it, and a few just might. At least it's another option which may get some students speaking a little more outside class. Hearing themselves is usually a good stimulus to get students interested in improving their pronunciation too. Remember, if they're unhappy with their performance, they can simply wipe it off and start again.

Obviously you won't have time to collect and listen to them all (taking home and playing 40 cassettes to your family is a short cut to divorce!), but you don't have to. Even if they go unmarked, the mere fact that students do them is good practice in itself. This works well when combined with memorisation. If students are trying to memorise a dialogue, a good way to test themselves is to do it 'live' onto cassette. Students can also send a 'cassette letter' to someone else in the class. At least they will have a lot of fun listening to them!

There are all sorts of activities students can do, depending on their level. As well as simply reading aloud, they can answer a series of written personal information questions about themselves. ◆ SEE PHOTOCOPIABLE PAGE 1

Any of the typical oral exam tasks can easily be done at home on cassette. Here are some examples.

- Describe a familiar place or person, e.g. your room, the view from your bedroom window, your mother, favourite star, boyfriend/girlfriend, etc.
- Describe a personal experience, e.g. last weekend, last summer, etc.
- An oral diary: tell the cassette what you did each day.
- Describe your routine or plans for the evening/weekend.
- Describe a picture.
- Describe the difference between two similar pictures.
- Narrate a picture story.
- Describe what's missing from a torn photo or picture.
- Giving directions, e.g. from their room to the street.
- Record a message for another student and give it to him/her next lesson, etc.

8 Phone a friend

Any question/answer exchange which is suitable for pairwork can also be done on the phone. Students can phone a partner and ask five questions, complete a form, decide what they're going to do tonight, etc. But beware: doing this too often may result in complaints from parents about their phone bill!

9 Teach your parents

If you're teaching younger children, a nice homework activity is to ask them to teach their parents the chorus or a verse of a song. Teenagers with interested parents can sometimes be persuaded to do the same, or else they can teach their parents a lexical set or series of useful phrases, e.g. parts of the body, travel phrases, etc. By asking them to try to do this, you can find out quite a lot about the kind of support your students are getting at home.

10 Grab a tourist!

The huge growth in world tourism has meant that most towns and cities now have plenty of foreign visitors, many of whom speak English. Tell your students to look out for them and try to help, e.g. with directions. For safety's sake, ensure that students only ever do this in groups, however.

As you can see from the above, oral homework can also be less boring and mechanical than many of the more traditional tasks. It at least provides some variety and balance to the skills students can practise.

Finally, a few general points to remember about homework.

- As we saw in Chapter 1, it's vital to define our objectives and goals to students. One simple way to do this is to tell students exactly which words they need to learn and revise from each lesson for homework.

- If you want students to take homework seriously, don't always set it at the last minute just after the bell has gone and students have started to pack up and leave! Give it emphasis by setting it at natural points during a lesson, making sure everybody notes down what they have to do.

- Equally important is to include homework performance as part of students' evaluation. The easiest way is to give a subjective impression mark from 0 to 4 for how often you think they've done it, e.g.

> 0 = never
> 1 = hardly ever
> 2 = sometimes
> 3 = regularly
> 4 = always

However, if you've got a lot of students and can't quite remember who exactly has done what, this can lead to arguments between students about their different marks. In this case, you could keep a 'homework register'. Tick or cross it each lesson for those who have/haven't done it, and give an individual annual mark, e.g. up to 25% of their annual total. Remind students regularly that they can fail the course if they don't do it.

- To save wasting excess class time, vary the way you check whether they've done it, e.g. ask for a show of hands of those who have done it, walk round quickly so they can show you their books, collect it in occasionally (even if only to see rather than mark it). Performance usually improves dramatically if you keep this up.

TASK

Look back at the activities above. Tick the ones that you're using already. Then choose one of the ideas that you haven't ticked and try it next week. Better still, persuade a colleague to try the same idea and then compare notes to see how it went.

CHAPTER 14

Oral evaluation

In many ways, this is the most important aspect of all. None of the ideas in the previous chapters is likely to be really successful unless speaking is part of the 'test'. If you ask students to speak regularly in class but then fail to reward them for this effort, you're making life difficult for yourself. Our students won't take speaking seriously if 'passing' or 'failing' depends only on their mark in a written exam. Students will only be encouraged to speak and so try to practise and improve if it's included in their evaluation.

This means you have to find a way to give occasional oral tests. Although time-consuming and sometimes difficult to arrange, especially with larger classes, they're often much less work than devising and writing traditional tests, which can take ages. They're also very motivating for students.

 **TASK** For a minute, BRAINSTORM all the reasons why you can't, don't or haven't given your students oral tests and oral marks. Then read the options below and see if you think they're feasible.

1 Continuous assessment

It's relatively easy to give an individual mark, e.g. from 1 to 5 or A to E for general willingness and ability to speak in class each term. Tell students that this will count as, e.g. 25 to 50% of their annual evaluation. Even if it may only be an impressionistic and often generous mark, the fact that students know their oral performance in class does count, and that they're being assessed all the time, will motivate those who want to pass the course to try to talk more.

If you do this, remind the class regularly that you're assessing their effort and performance. Tell students their mark at the end of each term, and encourage those who could do better to try harder next term.

An alternative way to do this is to give a mark from 1 to 5 or A to E for specific activities, once or twice a term (e.g. ROLEPLAY, a speaking game ◆ SEE PAGE 68, retelling a picture story ◆ SEE PHOTOCOPIABLE PAGE 4, or just pairwork questions and answers from prompts ◆ SEE PHOTOCOPIABLE PAGE 1.) To mark them, position yourself in the middle of the class to monitor, hear and mark the maximum number of students at once. Use the marking grid on page 79 to help you.

Note: Marking students while they work in groups can substantially cut the time required. Always tell students when they're being marked on their performance.

2 Short oral interviews

If feasible, interview students individually for three or four minutes, if necessary over two classes. Have a list of questions ready to ask. Meanwhile the rest of the class can:

… revise together quietly, knowing their turn is coming soon
… do the homework
… complete anything not yet done from their coursebooks or workbooks
… do a written test, written exercises or a composition
… work on a computer or in a language laboratory if available
… read a graded reader.

Alternatively, perhaps you could try to persuade a colleague to monitor the rest of your class or combine his/her class with the rest of yours in one room while you interview students in another.

It's a good idea to give the whole class either a list of specific questions they have to answer or general topics to prepare several weeks before you intend to test them. ◆ SEE THE LIST BELOW, OR PHOTOCOPIABLE PAGE 1 This defines the 'core' which all students are expected to know to pass the course whatever their level.

It's especially useful for weaker or less motivated students to remind them each week that they have to learn the questions and devise and memorise their answers or they won't pass the test. Even though they won't know exactly which questions/topics you'll choose, it should motivate them to practise a bit more both in and out of class.

Note: Interviewing students in pairs, asking them to discuss pictures, or do an INFORMATION-GAP activity together can save a lot of time.

Some suggested questions for oral tests

Use a mixture of direct questions and *Tell me about ...*, e.g. for elementary students:

Direct questions	Tell me about ...
1 *Where do you live?*	*your house*
2 *Do you like learning English? Why (not)?*	*your family*
3 *Where and when were you born?*	*your last holiday*
4 *How do you get to school?*	*your plans for (tomorrow)*
5 *How long does it take?*	*your typical morning/weekend*
6 *What are you doing (tonight)?*	*your favourite place*
7 *What are you going to do (at the weekend)?*	*your favourite clothes*
8 *What did you do last night?*	*your free time*
9 *Where were you at (3.00 p.m. yesterday)?*	*your hobbies*
10 *Have you ever been to (Britain)?*	*etc.*
11 *How often do you (go to the cinema)?*	
12 *What was the weather like yesterday?*	
13 *What do you do at weekends?*	
14 *What time do you usually (go to bed)?*	

3 Marking oral tests

Marking an oral test is always very subjective. Try giving marks as follows:

1 to 5 marks for FLUENCY and vocabulary range
1 to 5 marks for ACCURACY of grammar and pronunciation.

Explain this system to your class in L1 with some examples, e.g.

- A student who speaks easily, pronounces reasonably and says a lot without too many grammatical mistakes would score 5 for FLUENCY + 5 for ACCURACY = 10 marks.

- A student who uses a lot of words with a lot of mistakes but who can still be understood would score 4 + 3 = 7 marks.

- A student who says little, uses very few words, but doesn't make many mistakes would score 1 + 4 = 5 marks.

- A student who says virtually nothing and can't really be understood would score no marks.

When marking several students at once, a good idea is to use a simple grid so you can note individual scores easily and quickly, e.g.

NAME: *Amparo*	0	1	2	3	4	5
FLUENCY	—	—	—	—	✓ —	—
ACCURACY	—	—	—	✓ —	—	—
NAME: *Miguel*	0	1	2	3	4	5
FLUENCY	—	—	—	✓ —	—	—
ACCURACY	—	—	—	—	✓ —	—
NAME: *Maribel*	0	1	2	3	4	5
FLUENCY	—	—	✓ —	—	—	—
ACCURACY	—	✓ —	—	—	—	—
NAME:	0	1	2	3	4	5
FLUENCY	—	—	—	—	—	—
ACCURACY	—	—	—	—	—	—

Most teachers don't give oral tests because they think they have too many students, not enough time, or they don't know how. Of course, the more students you have, the harder it is, but it's never impossible. Oral tests really can be less time-consuming than writing, copying and marking your own more traditional tests. They're also different from the norm and can be much more motivating for students.

What alternative is there if we're really going to start teaching students to speak? Think back to your own experience as a language student at school. Would you have learned to speak more if you had been tested as above?

◆ FOR MORE IDEAS SEE *EVALUATING YOUR STUDENTS* IN THE SAME SERIES

T A S K

If you've never given your students an oral test, try playing the speaking game (PHOTOCOPIABLE PAGE 13) in groups of four. (If it's too difficult as it is, photocopy the board, then blank out and change the topics to simpler ones that your students can manage to talk about for thirty seconds.) Once they start playing, position yourself in the middle of the class and fill in a marking grid like the one above for each student. Allow a whole lesson for this and tell students that you're going to give a mark for their performance.

Where do we go from here?

There's no magic formula that will immediately make students start speaking in English. However, if we accept the assumption that speaking hasn't usually been taught successfully by traditional methods, some change of emphasis is needed. Instead of rushing through new grammatical structures just to satisfy the syllabus, if possible, we need to slow down a little to make time for students to assimilate, use and feel confident with the language we're teaching. Essentially, this means teaching less and revising and extending more than many school syllabuses now allow for. This has the following implications.

- The syllabus for each school year may have to be reduced so the students have less new language to learn and more time to practise and remember what they're supposed to be able to say. The activities in this book are often alternative ways of introducing and practising language, not additions to a busy timetable, and will help you to enable this to happen.

- Exams also have to accommodate and encourage speaking (and listening too).

- Classroom activities need to be more varied to allow enough practice, revision and extension, without boring students. Students need to re-use the words they're supposed to know in enough different contexts for them to 'stick'.

Perhaps we should all think about a 'core' **spoken** syllabus of, e.g. 100–200 words per year during primary and secondary school. If it were agreed that students **must** learn these words and phrases each year, no matter what else they learned, it would make a huge difference and we wouldn't have to 'start again' with speaking at the beginning of each school year.

1 Look carefully at your school syllabus, e.g. for Year 1. Is there anything there that you never really have time to teach properly? Or anything which is non-essential and would be better done in Year 2 to allow more time for speaking in Year 1? What do your colleagues think?

2 Teachers often complain but sometimes focus on the wrong things. In teaching speaking as in teaching anything else, think about your daily complaints and make a chart like this:

PROBLEMS	
which I might be able to do something about	which I really, really can't do anything about

Check that you're sure none of the items in the second column really belongs in the first. Try to look at them from every conceivable perspective, not just your own. With your colleagues, BRAINSTORM even the craziest possibilities, just in case. Then focus only on those from the first column you **can** affect. It's one way to stay sane as a teacher!

I would love to have been exposed to some of the techniques in this book at school and I hope you would too, at least enough to want to try a few of them out for yourself. Enjoy your teaching!

1 First year oral syllabus

SEE PAGE 8

PERSONAL

What/name?	What/phone number?
How/spell it?	Where/study?
Where/from?	Where/live?

IN YOUR FREE TIME

What sports/play?	How often/go to the cinema?
What magazines or comics/read?	What/like doing after school?
What kind of music/like?	What/like doing at weekends?
How often/go swimming?	

DESCRIBE YOUR HOME

/live in a flat or a house?	your bedroom?
How many bedrooms/ there?	/there any posters or photos in your bedroom?
/there a TV or a cassette player in	/there any toy shops or parks near you?

EVERY DAY

What time/usually get up?	How many hours a day/watch TV?
What/usually have for breakfast?	What time/go to bed?
/do a lot of sport?	How many hours a night/sleep?

WHAT HAVE YOU GOT?

a bike/skateboard?	any skates?
a computer/walkman?	any brothers/sisters?
any videos/CDs?	any pets?
any computer games?	any new clothes?

WHAT CAN YOU DO?

/play the guitar or another instrument?	/ski or swim?
/sing or dance well?	/touch your nose with your tongue?
/ride a horse or bike?	/whistle?
/skate?	

WHICH DO YOU PREFER? WHY?

/chocolate or strawberry ice cream?	/travelling by train or bus?
/milk or fruit juice?	/basketball or football?
/the summer or the winter?	/short or long hair?
	/Saturday or Sunday?

DESCRIBE A FRIEND

What/his or her name?	/tall/thin/good-looking?
Where/live?	What colour hair (eyes) /got?
How old/?	
/study English?	What/like doing?

WHAT DO YOU THINK OF...? WHY ?

(a singer or group)	(a school subject)
(a teacher)	(a computer game)
(a sports team)	(a TV programme)

TIME

What/the time?	Which/your favourite month?
What day/it today?	
What/the date today?	Which/your favourite season?
When/your birthday?	

THE PAST (BE)

When/born?	/at home yesterday evening?
Where/born?	
Where/last Saturday?	/late for school last week?
Where/last Sunday?	

PAST SIMPLE

/use a computer yesterday?	morning?
What/do last night?	/have breakfast this morning?
/see a film last weekend?	What/do last weekend?
What time/get up this	Where/go for your last holiday?

NOW

How/feeling?	What/your brother/ sister/aunt/uncle doing now?
What/wearing today?	
What/the teacher wearing?	What/your parents/ grandparents doing now?
What book/reading at the moment?	
What/doing now?	

WHAT ARE YOU GOING TO DO?

What/do after class?	/go away this weekend?
/watch TV tonight?	/visit your grandparents this weekend?
What/have for dinner tonight?	Where/go for your next holiday?
What/do tomorrow?	

Helping Students to Speak, © Paul Seligson, 1997

SEE PAGE 15

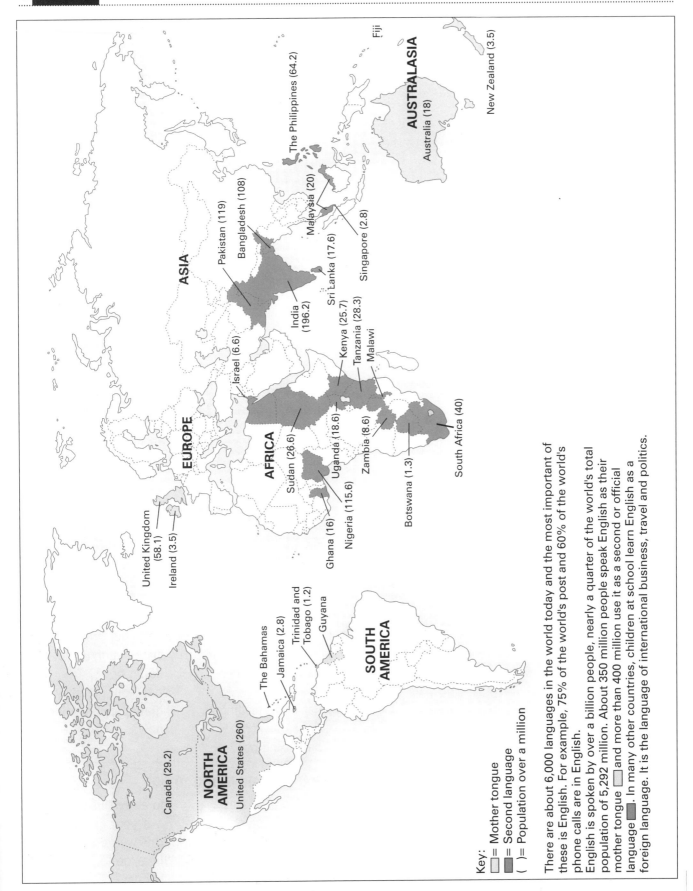

The Philippines (64.2)

Fiji

AUSTRALASIA

New Zealand (3.5)

Australia (18)

ASIA

Pakistan (119)

Bangladesh (108)

Malaysia (20)

Singapore (2.8)

Sri Lanka (17.6)

India (196.2)

Kenya (25.7)

Tanzania (28.3)

Malawi

Israel (6.6)

EUROPE

AFRICA

Sudan (26.6)

Uganda (18.6)

Zambia (8.6)

Botswana (1.3)

South Africa (40)

Ghana (16)

Nigeria (115.6)

United Kingdom (58.1)

Ireland (3.5)

The Bahamas

Jamaica (2.8)

Trinidad and Tobago (1.2)

Guyana

SOUTH AMERICA

Canada (29.2)

NORTH AMERICA

United States (260)

Key:

☐ = Mother tongue

▨ = Second language

( ) = Population over a million

There are about 6,000 languages in the world today and the most important of these is English. For example, 75% of the world's post and 60% of the world's phone calls are in English.

English is spoken by over a billion people, nearly a quarter of the world's total population of 5,292 million. About 350 million people speak English as their mother tongue ☐ and more than 400 million use it as a second or official language ▨. In many other countries, children at school learn English as a foreign language. It is the language of international business, travel and politics.

A Translate and learn these phrases. Use them in class.

YOUR LANGUAGE

Excuse me!

Can you help me, please?

How do you say ... in English?

spell ...?

pronounce ...?

Sorry?/Pardon?

Could you say that again?

Could you write that on the board, please?

What's the opposite of ...?

difference?

past tense of ...?

What does ... mean?

I'm sorry. I don't understand.

know.

remember.

Is this right or wrong?

Which page?

Have you got a ..., please?

Here you are.

Can I go to the toilet, please?

Sorry I'm late.

See you on (Monday)!

Have a nice weekend!

B Translate and learn these phrases to help you speak English together.

YOUR LANGUAGE

Can I borrow ..., please?

Can you pass ..., please?

That's/That isn't mine.

Just a moment, please.

We haven't finished (yet).

Come on. Hurry up!

Whose turn is it?

It's my/your turn.

You go first.

What did he/she say?

It doesn't matter.

What do you mean?

What do you think?

What/How about you?

I'm not sure.

Perhaps./Maybe.

Let's ask the teacher.

COME ON! PLEASE SPEAK ENGLISH!

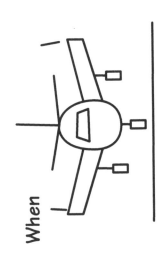

When

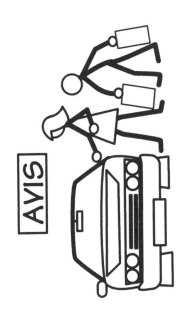

AVIS

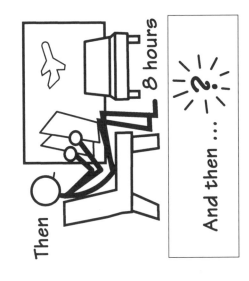

Then

And then …… 8 hours

TAXI

Then

AIRPORT

TAXI

When

BUREAU DE CHANGE

Yesterday afternoon

Then

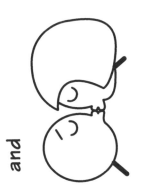

and

Helping Students to Speak, © Paul Seligson, 1997

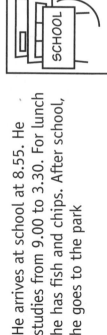
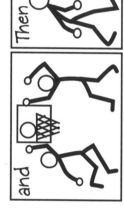

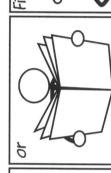

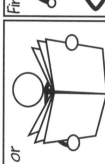

After that — **and** — **Then** — **Every Monday** 7.00

and — **8.00** — **and** — **and**

After school — **For lunch** — **9.00** / **3.30** — **8.55** — **SCHOOL**

7.30 — **and** — **Then** — **and**

Finally about 11.00 — **or** — **After dinner**

Every Monday ...... gets up at 7.00. Then he goes to the bathroom and has a shower. After that he goes downstairs to the kitchen

and has breakfast with his family. He has fruit juice and cereal. He leaves home at 8.00 and he goes to school by bus.

He arrives at school at 8.55. He studies from 9.00 to 3.30. For lunch he has fish and chips. After school, he goes to the park

and plays basketball with his friends. Then he goes home and does his homework. He has dinner at 7.30.

After dinner he watches TV, listens to the radio or reads. Finally, he goes to bed at about 11.00.

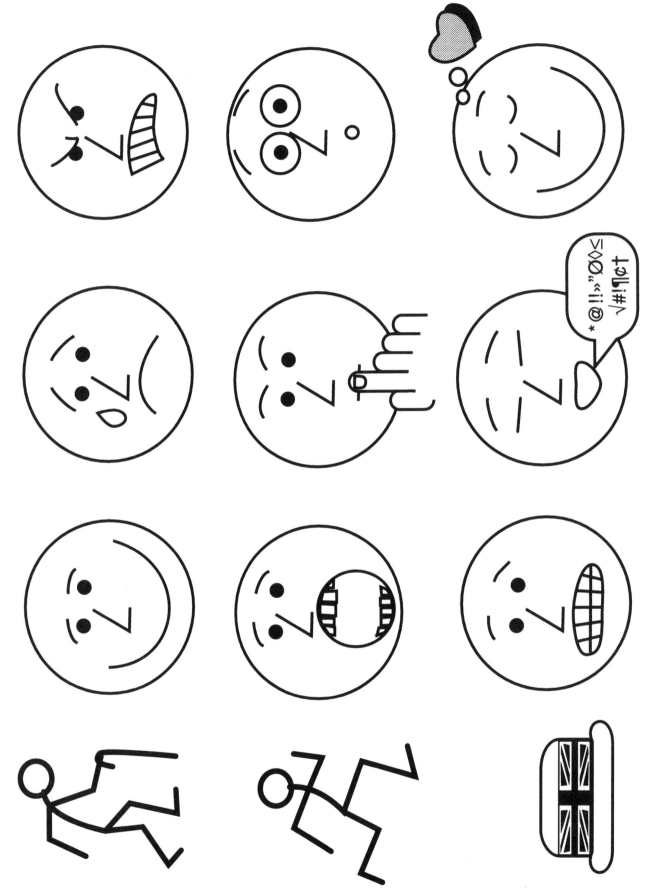

Helping Students to Speak, © Paul Seligson, 1997 **PHOTOCOPIABLE**

7 Spidergrams

SEE PAGE 58

1

HAVE
YOU
GOT...?

2

Where?

/ a good time?
/ fall in love?
/ buy any souvenirs?
/ any problems?

When?

YOUR
LAST
HOLIDAY

What / do in the | mornings?
afternoons?
evenings?

Who / with?

/ weather like?
/ food like?
/ people like?

How / get there?

Where / stay?
How long / stay?

 The number 2 spidergram includes the above items drawn around the central figure.

Helping Students to Speak, © Paul Seligson, 1997

Helping Students to Speak, © Paul Seligson, 1997 PHOTOCOPIABLE

SEE PAGE 63

1A

1B

2A

2B

Helping Students to Speak, © Paul Seligson, 1997

SEE PAGE 64

Find someone who ...	NAME	DETAILS
can	....	....
can't	....	....
likes	....	....
doesn't like	....	....
has got	....	....
hasn't got	....	....
would like to	....	....
.... when they leave school	....	....
went .... last weekend	....	....
didn't	....	....
has been to .... recently	....	....
hasn't been to	....	....
is going to .... soon	....	....
isn't going to .... this weekend	....	....
is the .... person in their family	....	....
....	....	....
....	....	....

Helping Students to Speak, © Paul Seligson, 1997

One day Junius du Pont met his friend, James Bond. He told Bond that he was having problems with a man called Auric Goldfinger. Every time they played cards together, Goldfinger always won. Du Pont was sure Goldfinger was cheating. So Bond watched them play. He saw that there was a beautiful girl on the balcony of the hotel. Her name was Jill and she was …

What was she doing?

… watching du Pont's cards and describing them to Goldfinger by radio. So Bond took the radio and made Goldfinger give du Pont a cheque for £100,000. Then Bond went home with Jill. Goldfinger wasn't happy and he …

What did he do?

… killed Jill by painting all her body with gold. Goldfinger thought Bond was a businessman looking for a job. He invited him to his house for dinner. There, Bond discovered that Goldfinger had a Rolls Royce made of …

What was his car made of?

… gold. Goldfinger loved gold. He was secretly buying a lot of gold in Britain. He was the richest man in the world. He was putting the gold in his special car and driving it to Switzerland. Soon there would be no gold in Britain! Goldfinger had a dangerous servant called Oddjob. A karate expert, he had a special hat made of metal which he used to kill people. Oddjob gave Bond an incredible demonstration and Bond was really afraid. For dinner, Goldfinger gave Oddjob …

What did he give him?

… a cat to eat (Oddjob's favourite food!). The next time Goldfinger went to Switzerland Bond followed him in his car. On the way, he met another girl called Tilly. Tilly was Jill's sister and she was also following Goldfinger. She wanted to …

What did she want to do?

… kill Goldfinger. But Oddjob caught them spying at Goldfinger's special gold factory in Switzerland. Goldfinger was really angry and told Oddjob to …

What did he tell him to do?

… kill them. But at the last minute, Goldfinger decided to make Bond and Tilly work for him. Goldfinger had a fantastic plan. He was going to rob Fort Knox, the bank with all the gold in America. He had a bomb to open the doors but he needed help to take away all the gold. So, he asked the top six gangsters in America to help him. He offered to pay them …

How much did he offer to pay them?

… two billion dollars each in gold. His plan was to poison the drinking water at Fort Knox and kill the 60,000 people who lived there. His plan was perfect, but when they were flying to Fort Knox, Bond …

What did Bond do?

… sent a message to the American police. He put a message under the toilet seat on the plane. When Goldfinger and his men arrived at Fort Knox, there were bodies everywhere. But, just before they could take the gold …

What happened?

… all the soldiers, who weren't really dead at all, suddenly got up and stopped them. Oddjob killed Tilly with his hat. Goldfinger escaped and caught Bond again. Now he knew Bond was a secret agent. Oddjob was sitting next to Bond on the plane. Goldfinger told him to kill Bond if he moved. But Bond had a knife in his shoe. He took it out and …

What did he do?

… broke the window next to Oddjob. The sudden change in pressure pulled Oddjob out of the window, but the plane started to go down. Goldfinger jumped on Bond. They had a hand-to-hand fight and finally …

What happened?

… Bond killed Goldfinger. But the plane crashed into the sea with Bond, Goldfinger's gold and all his men. The only ones who didn't die were …

Who didn't die in the crash?

… Bond and a gangster called Pussy Galore. Of course, she was very beautiful and she …

What did she do?

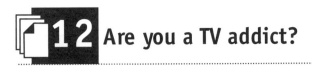

1 Have you got a TV?..............

2 How many TVs have you got at home?..............

3 Which room(s) is it/are they in?...

4 Do you know anybody who hasn't got a TV?..............

5 What do you think of the TV here?
   great ☐   good ☐   OK ☐   not very good ☐   terrible ☐

6 What's your favourite TV channel?...

7 How often do you watch TV ...?
   – before school ....
   – after school ....

8 Do you watch TV more ...?
   – during the week ☐
   – at the weekend ☐

9 Which person in your family watches TV more than everybody else?

   ....

10 Who in your family watches TV less than everybody else?

   ....

11 What's your favourite TV programme?.................................

12 What are the favourite programmes of the rest of your family?

   ....

13 What's the worst programme on TV?.................................

14 What's your favourite advert at the moment?.........................

15 Have you got a video?..............

16 Which programmes do you video?.................................

17 Do you ever rent videos?..............

18 Do you prefer watching TV or listening to the radio?.........................

19 Which do you do more: watch TV or listen to the radio?.........................

20 How many remote controls have you got?..............

Helping Students to Speak, © Paul Seligson, 1997 **PHOTOCOPIABLE**

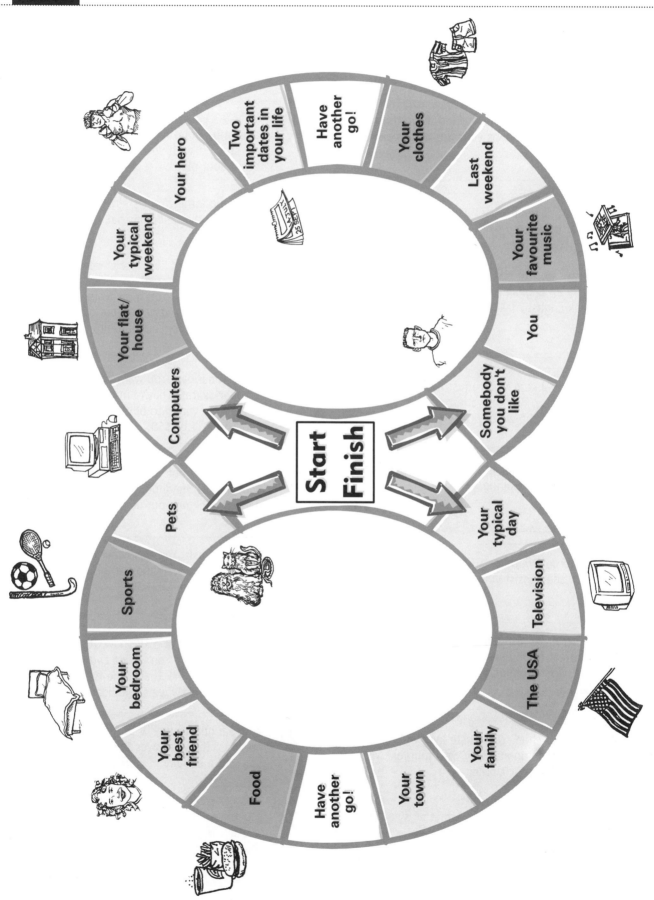

The speaking game board with the following spaces:

Start / Finish

Two important dates in your life · Have another go! · Your clothes · Last weekend · Your favourite music · You · Somebody you don't like · Your hero · Your typical weekend · Your flat/house · Computers · Pets · Sports · Your bedroom · Your best friend · Food · Have another go! · Your town · Your family · The USA · Television · Your typical day

1 A You're a tourist in England. You don't like English food. You're very, very hungry. Ask somebody in the street for help.

1 B You're English. You're walking down the street when a tourist stops you. You only speak English.

2 A You've left your school bag on the bus. It's full of things. Go to the police station. Tell the police officer.

2 B You're an English police officer. You only speak English. Take all A's details.

3 A You're in a café. You've just had lunch. It's time to pay. But you've left your purse at home. Call the waiter.

3 B You're an English waiter in a café. A wants to leave without paying.

4 A You've got toothache. Go to the dentist's. Show the dentist your bad tooth.

4 B You're an English dentist. You hate teenagers. You treat them but only if they eat healthy food. A is a foreign student who comes to see you.

5 A You're B's child. Your uncle lives in New York. You want to go and stay with him for two weeks. Ask your mother.

5 B You're A's mother. You're afraid of flying. You don't want your children to fly.

6 A You're the older brother. You want to redecorate your bedroom. The problem is that you share it with your younger sister (B). Tell your father your plans.

6 B You're A's younger sister. You want to redecorate your bedroom. The problem is that you share it with your older brother. Tell your father your plans.

6 C You're the father. Your children want to redecorate the bedroom that they share.

7 A You're American. You want to buy a pair of skates. Your friend has an old pair to sell. Try to get a cheap price. You don't want to spend more than $45.

7 B You're American. You want to sell an old pair of roller-skates. They're in good condition. Your friend wants to buy them. Try to get a good price, e.g. $60.

8 A You're in bed but you can't sleep because your English neighbour is having a noisy party. Knock on your neighbour's door.

8 B You're English. You're having a quiet party. Suddenly your neighbour knocks on your door. Answer it.

9 A You're the host of a TV show. It's the end of the programme. You've got two guests. Invent a question to ask them. The first person to answer correctly wins a holiday in Florida.

9 B You're a guest on a TV programme. You're very nervous. If you answer the question correctly, you win a holiday in Florida.

9 C You're a guest on a TV programme. You're very excited. If you answer the question correctly, you win a holiday in Florida.

Glossary

ACCURACY   When you focus on the correct production of language, whether grammar, functions, vocabulary or pronunciation, and don't allow errors.

BLU-TACK   A sticky, plasticine-like substance used to stick posters on walls, FLASHCARDS on the board, etc.

BRAINSTORM   When you spend a few minutes thinking of as many words/phrases connected with a particular topic as possible, without trying to organise them.

CLOSED PAIRS   When the students are all speaking in twos, concentrating solely on each other.

CONTINUOUS ASSESSMENT   When you check your students' progress at several points through the year, not just in one, final, end-of-year test.

FLASHCARDS   Large cards with either a picture or a word (sometimes both), which the teacher holds up for the class to see. They are often used in drills as picture/word prompts.

FLUENCY   When you focus on how students are communicating during an activity, i.e. whether they are conveying their message successfully, without correcting every little error they make.

FOLLOW-UP QUESTIONS   Secondary questions that can be asked during drills, Find someone who … exercises, etc. so students really communicate, e.g. if they're asking *Where do you live?*, questions may be *Is it a house or a flat? Do you like it there?*, etc.

INFORMATION GAP   An activity where students have different information from each other and have to put it together in order to solve a 'problem'.

MINGLE   Students move around the class, asking as many other students as possible the same question(s).

OPEN PAIRS   When two students are doing a pairwork exercise with the rest of the class listening.

OPINION GAP   An activity where students are likely to have different opinions and need to discuss them.

PROJECT   Activities which involve students doing some research and compiling information, pictures, etc. about a topic.

RANK   To put words/phrases/ideas in order from first to last according to given criteria, e.g. the biggest, best, etc.

ROLEPLAY   Any activity where students have to imagine themselves in a particular situation or character, e.g. a police officer and a criminal.

SCHWA   The schwa /ə/ is the most common vowel sound in English. It is the unstressed sound in words such as **a**bout, comput**e**r and fath**e**r.

SENTENCE STEMS   The beginnings of sentences/phrases which can be used as prompts in drills, ROLEPLAYS, etc.

SKELETON PROMPTS   The content words (e.g. nouns and verbs) of a sentence/question provided as prompts in drills, e.g. *Where/live? What/name?*

SPIDERGRAM   A way of organising vocabulary or ideas. The central theme/word is in a circle which has several 'legs' extending from it, which end in related words/phrases. See PHOTOCOPIABLE PAGE 7.

STORYBOARDING   Building up a dialogue or text from nothing (or almost nothing) just by indicating the number of words and proper names. Students guess words and gradually build up the text.

SWITCHING   The ability to move freely between two languages and use them both competently.

Further reading

Granger, C *Play Games with English* (1, 2 and 3) Heinemann 1993
A useful, fun range of games that students can play and complete together to practise speaking.

Hadfield, J *Communication Games: Elementary* (1984), *Intermediate* (1986) and *Advanced* (1990) Addison Wesley Longman
Photocopiable speaking games, some of which are very good.

Kenworthy, J *Teaching English Pronunciation* Addison Wesley Longman 1989
The best general introduction to teaching pronunciation.

Oxenden, C and Seligson, P *English File 1 & 2 (Teacher's Books)* OUP 1996
As well as an easy-to-copy flashcard presentation for all the main low-level structures, these both contain 60 photocopiable speaking activities.

Ur, P *Grammar Practice Activities* CUP 1988
Full of good, practical ideas to drill most structures.

Index of activities and topics

(numbers in brackets refer to photocopiable pages)

Key The answer to the task on page 64 is that all of the activities are suitable.